2/4/2014

Written 1997

published 2013

2013

WHAT I LEARNED
LOSING A
MILLION DOLLARS

WHAT I LEARNED LOSING A MILLION DOLLARS

JIM PAUL AND BRENDAN MOYNIHAN

Columbia Business School
Publishing

Columbia University Press
Publishers Since 1893
New York   Chichester, West Sussex
cup.columbia.edu
Copyright © 2013 Brendan Moynihan
All rights reserved

Library of Congress Cataloging-in-Publication Data

Paul, Jim.
What I learned losing a million dollars / Jim Paul and Brendan Moynihan.
    p.   cm.—(Columbia Business School publishing)
Includes bibliographical references.
ISBN 978-0-231-16468-9 (cloth : alk. paper)—ISBN 978-0-231-53523-6
(e-book)
1. Commodity exchanges.   2. Speculation.   3. Speculation—
Psychological aspects.   I. Moynihan, Brendan.   II. Title.

HG6046.P38 2013
332.64'5092—dc23

2012040403

∞
Columbia University Press books are printed on permanent and durable
acid-free paper.
This book is printed on paper with recycled content.
Printed in the United States of America

c 10 9 8 7 6 5 4 3 2 1

COVER IMAGE: ©Shutterstock
COVER DESIGN: Noah Arlow

CONTENTS

Foreword vii
Preface to the Columbia Edition xi
Preface xiii

PART ONE Reminiscences of a Trader 1

1 From Hunger 5
2 To the Real World 11
3 Wood That I Would Trade 32
4 Spectacular Speculator 40
5 The Quest 59

PART TWO Lessons Learned 67

6 The Psychological Dynamics of Loss 73
7 The Psychological Fallacies of Risk 85
8 The Psychological Crowd 100

CONTENTS

PART THREE Tying It All Together 115

9 Rules, Tools, and Fools 117

Conclusion 145
Postscript 152

Appendix 161
Notes 163
Bibliography 169

FOREWORD

Jack Schwager

One paradox I often pose to my audiences in talks about the elements of successful trading concerns the dichotomy in human thinking as it relates to trading versus everything else. Specifically, I use the following example: No sane person would walk into a bookstore (assuming you could still find one these days), go to the medical section, find a book on brain surgery, read it over the weekend, and then believe he could walk into an operating room on Monday morning and perform successful brain surgery. The operative word here is "sane." Yet how many people do you know who would think that it is perfectly reasonable to walk into a bookstore, go the investment section, find a book with a title like *How I Made a Million Dollars Trading Stocks Last Year*, read it over the weekend, and then start trading Monday morning and expect to beat the professionals at their own game. Why this dichotomy in thinking?

The foregoing paradox is one that I believe has a satisfactory answer. Trading, as far as I know, is the only endeavor in which the rank amateur has a 50/50 chance of being right. Why? Because there are only two things you could do in trading: you can buy or you can sell. And, as a consequence, some portion of clueless beginners will get it right simply by chance—*for a while*. This potential for temporary success by pure luck beguiles people into thinking that trading is a lot easier than it is. The potential for even temporary success doesn't exist in any other profession. If you have never trained as a surgeon, the probability of your performing successful brain surgery is zero. If you have never picked up a violin, your chances of playing successful solo violin in front of the New York Philharmonic are zero. It is just that trading has this quirk that allows some people to be successful temporarily without true skill or an edge—and that fools people into mistaking luck for skill.

Jim Paul thought that his early success in the markets was caused by his being smart or maybe by his willingness to break the rules. He didn't realize that his heady run was based on luck until he had lost all his profits and a good deal more. And Paul would be the first to admit that his winning streak was a matter of luck even though it lasted for years. This conclusion is unavoidable because his deficiency as a trader made a total loss inevitable. As he readily acknowledges, even if had not lost all his money when he did, it would merely have postponed this ultimate outcome, perhaps to a point in time when his loss would have been that much greater.

The truth is that trading, both successful and unsuccessful, is more about psychology than tactics. As Jim Paul ultimately learns through a very expensive lesson taught by the market, successful trading is not about discovering a great strategy for making money but rather a matter of learning how to lose. From the research he conducts following his catastrophic experience in the markets, Paul realizes that winning traders differ radically, using approaches that often contradict one another. What winning traders share, however, is that they all understand that losing is part of the game, and they all have learned how to lose. By losing everything, Paul becomes an expert on losing, and it is only then that he can become a winning trader rather than a temporarily lucky one.

There is more to be learned from Jim Paul's true story of failure than from a stack of books promising to reveal the secret formula for success. Not only that: *What I Learned Losing a Million Dollars* is a much more entertaining read. Although the book can be read simply as a humorous and breezy tale, readers should not lose sight of the

fact that this compact volume is filled with a wealth of trading wisdom and insights. It cost Paul a fortune to learn these lessons; the
reader has the opportunity to benefit from this knowledge for the
mere cost of a book—a true bargain.

PREFACE TO THE COLUMBIA EDITION

Since this book was first published, nearly twenty years ago, a lot has changed in the world of trading. Open outcry is nearly dead, exchanges have merged, and newfangled instruments have been created—some of which generated losses that brought the global financial market to its knees.

One thing that has not changed over the past twenty years is the decision-making mistakes that traders and investors make in the markets. Whether you are a professional managing other people's money or an individual managing your own money, you are susceptible to these mistakes—if not on the same scale of operations. Since the book's first printing, we have witnessed some colossal risk-management disasters. For example, Nick Leeson of Barings Bank lost 827 million pounds ($1.4 billion) in 1995 betting on the Japanese stock market. Toshihide Iguchi of Daiwa Bank lost $1.1 billion the same year. Yasuo Haminaka, a.k.a. Mr. Copper, of Sumitomo lost $2.6 billion trading copper in 1996. Then there was John Rusnak at Allfirst Bank, who lost $691 million in 2002 trading currencies. Chen Juilin of China Aviation Oil Corporation lost $550 million in 2005 trading jet-fuel futures (It was a spectacular fall from grace for the "King of Aviation Oil.") And Jerome Kerviel of Societe Generale dropped a stunning 4.9 billion euros ($7.4 billion) between 2006 and 2008 in equity derivatives.

These highly publicized cases, and others, riveted media, management, and academic attention on the strategies and controls of the risk-management business. While the many postmortems offered valuable lessons, mostly in the areas of internal controls and hedge-strategy selection, these autopsies have largely overlooked what went on inside the minds of the individual traders actually pulling the trigger on the trades. While lax controls may have *enabled* these losses to occur and questionable hedging strategies may have *contributed* to the losses, neither factor *caused* the losses; traders did. And to understand and prevent losses we need to get inside the mind of the individual. This book does that. I use Jim Paul's story as a parable to point out the three biggest mistakes that investors and traders make every day in the markets. These have not changed and never will. The mistakes are timeless, and so are the lessons for avoiding them. I've talked to hundreds of traders and investors since the book's publication, and to a person they've agreed with the premise of the book and the lessons it holds. This is because all of us lose money as some point; and the book simply identifies the mental processes, behavioral characteristics, and emotions that lead us into those losses. Then it offers a prescription for avoiding those processes, characteristics, and emotions—and the losses that accompany them. May the lessons teach and the stories entertain.

PREFACE

Books can generally be categorized into one of three groups: education, entertainment, or reference. Education books teach us; entertainment books amuse us; and reference books inform us. This book combines education with entertainment to make it easier to recall the lessons by remembering the story. In that sense, this book is a parable: a simple story illustrating important lessons. From the story of the little boy who cried wolf to the story of the emperor's new clothes, parables have been used to convey lessons that apply to many aspects of life. Similarly, in this book the story is about a commodities trader, but its lessons apply to stock-market and bond-market investors, as well as all types of business people: entrepreneurs, managers, and CEOs.

The moral of the story you are about to read is: Success can be built upon repeated failures when the failures *aren't* taken personally; likewise, failure can be built upon repeated successes when the successes *are* taken personally. Thomas Edison failed roughly 10,000 times before finding the right filament to make an electric light bulb. The day his Menlo Park laboratory burned to the ground a reporter asked him what he was going to do. Edison responded, "Start rebuilding tomorrow." In part, Edison succeeded because he didn't take failures or losses personally. On the other hand, consider Henry Ford, who worked with and greatly admired Edison. Ford started in 1905 with nothing and in fifteen years had built the largest and most profitable manufacturing firm on the planet. Yet a few years later, this seemingly impregnable business empire was in shambles and would go on to lose money almost every year for the next two decades. Ford was known to stick uncompromisingly to his opinions; is it possible his company lost so much money because he took the successes personally and came to think he could do no wrong?

Personalizing successes sets people up for disastrous failure. They begin to treat the successes totally as a personal reflection of their abilities rather than the result of capitalizing on a good opportunity, being at the right place at the right time, or even being just plain lucky. They think their mere involvement in an undertaking guarantees success.

This phenomenon has been called many things: hubris, overconfidence, arrogance. But the way in which successes become personalized and the processes that precipitate the subsequent failure have never been clearly spelled out. That is what we have set out to do. This book is a case study of the classic tale of countless entrepreneurs: the risk taker who sees an opportunity, the idea that clicks, the intoxicating growth, the errors, and the collapse. Our case is that of a trader, but as with all case studies and parables the lessons can be applied to a great many other situations. These lessons will help you whether you are in the markets or in business. The two areas have more in common than one might suppose. Warren Buffettt, the richest man in America, is quoted on the cover of *Forbes*'s 1993 edition of the "400 Richest People in America": "I am a better investor because I am a businessman, and I'm a better businessman because I'm an investor." If the elements of success can be transferred between the markets and business, the elements of failure can too.

We could study a hypothetical series of successes to demonstrate how success becomes personalized and then how a loss follows, but you are more likely to remember and learn the lessons if they are presented in anecdotes about a real person and a really big loss. How big? The collapse of a fifteen-year career and the loss of over one million dollars in a mere seventy-five days.

WHY A BOOK ON LOSING?

Almost without exception, anyone who has participated in markets has made some money. Apparently people have at least some knowledge about making money in the markets. However, since most people have lost more money than they have made, it is equally apparent that they lack knowledge about not losing money. When they do lose, they buy books and attend seminars in search of a new method of how to make money since that last method was "obviously defective." They are like racing fans making the same losing bet on an instant replay. Investors' bookshelves are filled with Horatio Alger stories of rags-to-riches millionaires. Sometimes these books are read solely for entertainment, but more often than not they are read in an attempt to learn the secret of how the millionaires made their fortunes, particularly when those millions were made by trading in the markets. Most of these books are of the "how-to" genre, from James Brisbin's 1881 classic *The Beef Bonanza: How to Get Rich on the Plains* to modern-day versions of how to get rich in the market: *How to win in the market . . .* , *How to use what you already know to make . . .* , *How to apply the winning strategies . . .* , *How to make a million dollars in the market before breakfast*. We've all read them, but if the "how-to" books were that beneficial, we'd all be rich.

A review of the investment and trading literature reveals very little written about losing money. When something has been written on this topic, it's usually a sensationalistic, unauthorized tell-all biography or tabloid-like exposé that panders to people who delight in the misfortune of others. Personality-journalism books are definitely read for entertainment, not as an attempt to learn from the subject's mistakes. Losing has received only superficial coverage in most books on the markets; they raise the subject, stress its importance, and then leave it dangling.

What I Learned Losing a Million Dollars is a light treatise on the psychology of losing and is intended for investors, speculators, traders, brokers, and money managers who have either lost money or would like to protect against losing what they've made. Most discussions of the psychological aspects of the markets focus on behavioral psychology or psychoanalysis (i.e., sublimation, regression, suppression, anger, self-punishment). This isn't to say such books aren't instructive; it's just that most people find it hard to digest and apply the information presented in those books. Other books use hypothetical character sketches to make their points while others simply compile a list of old saws about losses. This book, on the other hand, entertains and educates you on the psychology of market losses in layman's terms, anecdotally, through the story of a trader who actually lost over a million dollars in the market.

The first part of the book is Jim Paul's personal odyssey of an unbroken string of successes that took him from dirt-poor country boy to jet-setting millionaire and member of the Executive Committee at the Chicago Mercantile Exchange before a devastating $1.6 million loss brought him crashing down. One of the premises of this book is that the rise sets up the fall; the winning sets up the losing. You can't really be set up for disaster without having it preceded by success. If you go into a situation in a neutral position, having neither successes nor failures beforehand, you acknowledge that your odds are maybe fifty-fifty; you may have a winner, you may have loser. But if you start from scratch and have a run of successes, you are setting yourself up for the coming failure because the successes lead to a variety of psychological distortions. This is particularly true if you have unknowingly broken the rules of the game and won anyway. Once that happens to you, you think that you are somehow special and exempt from following the rules.

The seeds of Jim's disaster were sown with his first job at the age of nine. His exposure to the outside world, money, and material things was the foundation for his career's sharp and quick ascent as well as its ultimate collapse. Repeated attempts to make the money back by speculating in the markets ended in failure and left Jim disillusioned. He set out on a quest to find out how the pros made money in the markets so he could follow their example. When you're sick you want to consult the best doctors; when you're in trouble you want the best lawyers; so Jim read all about the techniques of the professionals to learn their secret of making money. But this search left him even more disillusioned since he discovered that the masters made money not only in widely varying ways but also in ways that contradicted each other. What one market pro advocated, another ardently opposed. It finally occurred to him that studying losses, losing, and how not to lose was more important than studying how to make money.

The second part of the book presents the lessons Jim learned from his losing experience. Namely, there are as many ways to make money in the markets as there are people participating in the markets, but there are relatively few ways to lose money in the markets. People lose money in the markets either because of errors in their analysis or because of psychological factors that prevent the application of the analysis. Most of the losses are due to the latter. All analytical methods have some validity and make allowances for the times when they won't work. But psychological factors can keep you in a losing position and also cause you to abandon one method for another when the first one produces a losing position.

The third part of the book shows you how to avoid the losses due to psychological factors. Trading and investment mistakes are well known and easily understood but difficult to correct. What you need is not a long litany of complex psychological theories but a simple framework to help you understand, accept, and thereby avoid catastrophic losses. This book will help you recognize, identify, and avoid the pitfalls of investing, trading, and speculating.

So, why a book on losing? Because, there are as many ways to make money in the markets as there are participants but relatively few ways to lose, and despite all the books on how to make money in the markets, most of us aren't rich!

Brendan Moynihan
Nashville, TN
May 1994

WHAT I LEARNED
LOSING A
MILLION DOLLARS

PART ONE

REMINISCENCES OF A TRADER

Experience is the worst teacher. It gives the test before giving the lesson.

—UNKNOWN

I made $248,000. In one day, a quarter of a million dollars. The high was unbelievable. It's literally like you expect God to call up any minute and ask if it's okay to let the sun come up tomorrow morning.

I had a special desk that was a copper pedestal coming out from the floor, and on top of it was a giant 3′ x 6′ x 7″ piece of mahogany. The table-top looked like it was suspended in midair. The credenza was a matching piece of wood bolted to the wall, also looking like it was suspended in mid-air. When you walked into the office all you could see was carpet stretching out in front of you, a copper column rising up from the carpet, and two pieces of wood levitating in midair, defying gravity. And that is just what I thought I was doing: defying gravity. I sat down at my desk on the edge of my chair waiting for the market to open, ready to have another $50,000 day, and thinking life didn't get any better than this. I was right. It didn't.

The market opened down that morning and never traded higher than it did on that last Friday in August. It started down that Monday, and I proceeded to lose on average about $20,000 to $25,000 a day, every day, for months. The decline was relentless, with only occasional spasms to the upside. Fortunately, I started getting the clients out of the market. Most of the clients got out with some profit, some with small losses. Naturally, I didn't get out. I was in for the long pull. This was going to be the Big Trade. Kirby and I were going to make $10 million on this trade.

By the middle of October I was under water. I didn't know how far under I was, but I knew I'd lost most of my money. As the position got increasingly worse, I began to get margin calls. I'd wait a few days to see if the market rallied so I wouldn't have to meet the margin call. If it did, fine. If it didn't, I'd spend the next couple of days trying to borrow money from my friends. I'd be on margin call for two or three days at a time, but the brokerage firm's attitude was, "We know you're a big wheel. You're on the Board of Governors of the Exchange. You're on the Executive Committee. You're an officer of your firm, etc. We know you're good for the money."

The first week in November, I was under water big time: $200,000 or $300,000. I didn't even know how much it was. Bean oil had gone from 36 or 37 cents a pound down to 25 cents. So from the high in August, I was down $700,000 or $800,000. To make matters worse, I'd borrowed about $400,000 from my friends.

The firm finally, and mercifully, pulled the plug on me because I couldn't. On November 17, one of the senior managers from the brokerage firm came into my office and proceeded to liquidate all my positions.

I went from having everything on August 26 to nothing on November 17. However, I didn't intend to give up on trading. I viewed it like blackjack in the caddy pen: I wasn't going to quit playing, but I was going to quit losing.

I didn't lose that kind of money simply because of a faulty method of analysis. That may have played a role, but something else was going on to keep me in a losing position even to the point where I went into debt to hold onto it. That something was the psychological distortion accompanying a series of successes, drawing my ego into the market position and setting me up for the disastrous loss.

As mentioned in the preface, these same distortions afflicted Henry Ford and contributed to his company's downfall in the 1920s and 1930s. And these distortions continue to afflict businesses, managers, and CEOs today. For example, in 1993 management guru Peter F. Drucker wrote in the *Wall Street Journal* that "the past few years have seen the downfall of one once-dominant business after another: General Motors, Sears and IBM, to name just a few" and that "IBM's downfall was paradoxically caused by unique success."[1] Drucker has also said, "Success always obsoletes the behavior that achieved it." While some of the factors contributing to these downfalls were a function of the particular strategies the firms employed (Drucker called them the Five Deadly Business Sins), there were other factors that were a function individual managers' decision making. This book explores the latter factors.

Personalizing successes sets people up for disastrous failure. They begin to treat the success as a personal reflection rather than the result of capitalizing on a good opportunity, being at the right place at the right time, or even being just plain lucky. People begin to think their mere involvement in the undertaking guarantees success. Apparently, this is a common phenomenon. Listen to An Wang, founder of Wang Laboratories: "I find it somewhat surprising that so many talented people derail themselves one way or another during their lives . . . all too often a meteoric rise triggers a precipitous fall. People fail for the most part because they shoot themselves in the foot. If you go for a long time without shooting yourself in the foot, other people start calling you a genius."[2] Listen to Herb Kelleher, CEO of Southwest Airlines: "I think the easiest way to lose success is to become convinced that you are successful."[3] This "becoming convinced" is the process of personalizing achievements or successes. Learning to recognize and prevent that process is what this book is all about.

When I was a kid, my father told me there are two kinds of people in the world: smart people and wise people. Smart people learn from their mistakes and wise people learn from somebody else's mistakes. Anyone reading this book has a wonderful opportunity to become wise because I am now very, very smart. I learned a lot from the mistakes that led to a million-and-a-half-dollar loss in the market. But there is more to the story than the fantastic fall from the pinnacle of millionaire trader and member of the Executive Committee at the Chicago Mercantile Exchange. There is the almost fantasy-like ascent to the top that set the stage for the collapse.

1

FROM HUNGER

I got my first job when I was nine years old. One of my classmates was a caddy at a local country club near Elsmere, Kentucky. One day he asked me if I wanted to be a caddy too, and I said, "Sure." My parents thought it was a good idea since it would teach me the value of a dollar. I thought it was a great idea since I would get to keep the dollars.

This was the beginning of my love affair with money. As a result of working at the country club, I learned just how important money really was. It enabled people to have the nicer things in life, most of which I hadn't even known existed. My father was only making $4,000 or $5,000 a year as a surveyor back in the early 1950s, so we couldn't afford the nicer things in life.

Summit Hills was not a very fancy country club, but it was a country club and the people there had a lot more money than the people near where I lived did. So at the age of nine I became one of the only kids in my class at St. Henry's who knew that "Oldsmobiles are better." I used to caddy for Charlie Robkey. He didn't play golf very well, but he made a lot of money and had a beautiful car. Charlie would show up in his new Cadillac Eldorado convertible with the top down and his good-looking blond wife who had on a chiffon scarf sitting next to him. I would say to myself, "Self, I like what Charlie's got, and I think I want to do what Charlie's doing. I don't want to drive a

Chevrolet like my folks. I'd like to have an Eldorado like Charlie." I didn't even know what Charlie did for a living, and it didn't matter. Charlie made a lot of money and had many of the nicer things in life.

GOOSE NICKELS

As far as I could see, it wasn't what you did for a living that was important in life; it was how much you got paid for doing it. This idea was driven home not only by the members of the country club, like Charlie Robkey, but also by the other caddies. We all admired a guy by the name of Goose—Old Goose. He was about fourteen or fifteen, and that's old to a nine-year-old. We had a big area called the caddy pen where all the caddies would sit around waiting to go out on a round. We used to pitch nickels against a wall, and Goose was very good at pitching nickels. He could get those nickels to stop up against the wall almost every time. So while I was toting these big golf bags around for four hours to make two dollars, Goose was up there in the caddy pen pitching nickels. At the end of the day, Goose had more money than I did. I worked harder than Goose, but Goose had more money. He had the respect and admiration of everybody in the caddy pen—not because he could pitch nickels better than everyone else but because he had a lot of nickels. Making money became important to me, whether I made it by slow honest industry carrying golf bags or by quick strokes pitching nickels. It wasn't what you did; it was how much you made.

NO LITTLE LEAGUE

This view of the importance of money was also reinforced by my parents. They not only wanted me to learn the value of a dollar but to have a job and start making that dollar. Some of my friends from school were trying out for the Little League baseball team, and, naturally, I wanted to try out, too. When we got to the field, the coach asked each of us what position we wanted to try out for. I said, "Shortstop." I didn't know what a shortstop was or did, but it was the only position I'd heard my friends talk about. Besides, I was short and thought the name sounded neat. That was a mistake; every ball hit to me either rolled between my legs, glanced off my glove, or bounced off my head. But I could hit the ball. I hit many of the pitches over the outfielders' heads. Then I hit one directly at the coach who was pitching. I made the team . . . playing left field.

At our first game I hit a grand slam home run to win the game four to two. My expert fielding was responsible for the other team's two runs, as well as for getting my uniform dirty. Well, the uniform was a problem because I hadn't told my parents that I had gone out for tryouts and made the team. When I showed up at home that afternoon with a dirty baseball uniform for my mother to clean, I was told I had to quit. "Baseball isn't practical; caddying is. You make money caddying, not playing baseball." Thus ended my short-lived but illustrious baseball career, reinforcing my view that money was important.

So it was through my exposure to the country club and the caddy pen that I first learned about money and something about making it. I also learned that it was possible to make money playing blackjack, poker, and gin. By the time I was ten, I was playing nickel blackjack. Since money was important to me, I was very upset when I almost always lost at blackjack in the caddy pen. I was whining to Goose about it one day, and he told me that I was losing because he and the other guys were cheating. He showed me how he burned the first card on the deck, placing it face up on the bottom so that you couldn't tell the difference between the top and the bottom of the deck. He would pick up the old hands and place them on bottom, but rotate the deck as he needed the known cards on the bottom. I didn't stop playing blackjack, but I did stop losing.

After being exposed to this money culture at the country club, I wanted to get involved in what the people who had the money were involved in. I wanted to know the right people. So I ingratiated myself with the right people, like Johnny Meyer. Johnny Meyer was the club champion. I became Johnny's personal caddy, which is how I got out of Elsmere, Kentucky, the first time in my life. I went to Big Springs Country Club with Johnny in his big Chrysler convertible. He took me to Louisville to be his caddy when he played in the Kentucky State Amateur Championships. We drove from Cincinnati down to Louisville, and at thirteen years old I just thought that was the neatest thing in the world. I was in this cool car with this neat guy who was a great golfer, and I was going to a country club in another city. He was taking me because I was such a good caddy. It was only a seventy-mile trip, but for me that was a long way.

My involvement with the country-club set changed my perspective on the world and society. If I hadn't been involved, I never would have known about the nicer things in life. Where I grew up in Elsmere, if you weren't exposed to this "other life," you'd have never known it existed. It's the old situation where Joe Lunch Box is the happiest guy in the world. Joe Lunch Box is the guy who graduates from high school and gets a job at the local factory. He goes to work, tightens the four nuts on the left side of a V-8 engine, eats his lunch, tightens the four nuts on the left side of another V-8 engine, goes home, watches TV, and has a beer. He's happy because he doesn't know that Eldorados are neat, that chiffon scarves on the girl in the seat next to you are neat, and that McGregor golf clubs with the gold faces are the best and Spaulding Executives are second class. You want McGregor clubs with the gold faces. If you weren't exposed to this "other life," you didn't know it existed and you didn't know you were missing it.

The country club exposed me to the better things in life, and I wanted the better things. Well, that was a problem because once I learned about this "other life" and that it was better, I also knew that I was missing it. I was at a disadvantage to most of my peers because I wanted more than they even knew existed. I wanted to learn how to play golf. I wanted to be one of the guys caddies would come up to and say, "Good morning, Mr. Paul," just like I had to say, "Good morning, Mr. Robkey." I wanted to become one of *these* country-club guys, not one of those Joe Lunch Box guys.

Basically, what I learned at the country club was: It's not what you do for a living that's important. What's important is how much you get paid for doing it. I could work hard like Joe Lunch Box or I could work smart like Charlie Robkey.

While I believed it was true that what you got paid was more important that what you did, it was also true that certain high-paying jobs required some higher education. Joe Lunch Box only went through high school, whereas the Charlie Robkeys and the Johnny Meyers of the world went to college. I realized that in order for me to make serious money, I was going to have to get some kind of education. In order to get a reasonable education, I was going to have to pay for it. I needed money to get an education. To make money I had to have some money, so I always had some kind of job since I was nine years old. I was one of the few guys in St. Henry's High paying my way through school. It was a parochial school, and I had to go because my parents were strict Catholics and they said I had to go. But my folks didn't have enough money to pay the tab, so I paid for tuition, books, and clothes. This reinforced my sense of how important money was.

I caddied until I was about fifteen. During that time I also worked in the pro shop and gave golf lessons. After I stopped caddying, I ran a golf-driving range for a while. Next I worked in a restaurant busing tables, and then I worked in a service station. My senior year of high school I worked fifty-five hours a week in the service station. I'd get out of school at two p.m. and work from three to eleven p.m. five days a week and then eight to ten hours a day on Saturday and Sunday. My folks were very lenient about curfew the whole time I was growing up. I could spend my money and do whatever I wanted because I was working so hard. They really let me do whatever I wanted as long as I didn't get in trouble. My dad's attitude was: "If you screw up and get in trouble boy, I'm gonna . . ." My parents laid the ground rules, and I followed them.

Once you know what the rules are, it's easy; just follow the rules and win. Once I figured out what it took to get from point A to point B, I did the bare minimum of what it took to get the job done. I drove my teachers crazy because I did well at what I liked and I did poorly at what I didn't like. All you needed to pass was Cs, so most of the time I got Cs. I did just what it took to get by—unless I was interested. If

I liked the course, I'd get an A. Every report card I ever received had the same comment: "Does not work to potential." I really drove my teachers crazy. And to top it off, I was elected president of the student council. I was not the type of person the teachers thought should be president. They wanted one of their pet student types who didn't drink, drive fast, or otherwise screw around.

I had a lot of freedom since I had my own job, my own money, and my own car. I bought a '53 Mercury on my sixteenth birthday with my own money: $700 cash. Man, was it neat! A year later I sold it and bought a '56 Chevy, which was even neater. It wasn't an Eldorado, but it was neat. At seventeen years old in Elsmere, Kentucky, one of the biggest things in your life was your car—and did I ever have a car. I had the '56 Chevy lowered and shaved. I don't know if anybody will remember what shaved is, but that's when you take the emblems, the trim, and the hood ornament off the car, fill the holes with lead, and then repaint it. Then you lower it. I put a big V-8 engine in it and a Hurst speed shift in the floor. This '56 Chevy was hot! It was dark metallic blue with rolled and pleated leather seats and special carpet on the floor. So by the time I was seventeen, I thought I was well on my way to becoming "Mr. Paul" at the country club. I was working and making money, and I had a cool car with a pretty girlfriend in the seat next to me. Look out Mr. Robkey, here I come!

2

TO THE REAL WORLD

I sold the '56 Chevy to pay for college. Neither of my parents had been to college so it was sort of a big deal to them that I was going. I used the money from the car and my savings account to pay my way through college. The whole time I had been working, my parents had forced me to put 10 percent of whatever I made in a savings account that they controlled.

I was accepted to the University of Kentucky in 1961. At the time, state law mandated that if you graduated from a Kentucky accredited high school, you would be accepted to UK. The hard part was staying in once you got there. Since they didn't have room for every Kentucky high school graduate, they tried to flunk out as many students as possible in the first two semesters. The flunk-out course was freshman English. Early in my first semester someone explained that this was "the game," and I made sure they didn't flunk me out of school. I couldn't afford to fail because the only way I was going to get into a country club as "Mr. Paul" was to graduate from college. So I studied my tail off and made a B in freshman English. I finished the semester with a 2.6 grade-point average. All you needed to stay was a 2.0, and I made sure I stayed. Having survived that first crucial semester, I turned my attention to social life.

FRAT LIFE

Boy, was I in for a surprise when I tried to make it on the social scene. Everybody around me had more money than I did. They also all had Bass Weejuns. I didn't even know what a Bass Weejun was—it's a style of shoe. Everybody in Lexington wore Bass Weejuns. I had no money, no good clothes, and no Bass Weejuns. I didn't even have a suit. I bought my first suit when I was a senior in college, and my buddy Tommy Kron had to lend me the money to buy that. My folks were sending me ten dollars a week out of my "10-percent-of-everything-bank-account," and that was my spending money. When I left Elsmere, I was a pretty big wheel; I had a neat car, I was dating the head cheerleader, I was president of the student council, and so on. I had some status as a hometown boy, but when I got down to Kentucky as a freshman, I was from hunger again.

I was just another freshman in Kincaid Hall, a nobody. Socially, there is nothing more pitiful than a freshman boy in college. You are totally worthless. The freshman girls are all looking at the sophomore and junior guys, so the freshman boys just hang around with one another drinking beer and telling stories about how good it used to be in high school.

After six months of this, I decided that if I were in a fraternity things would pick up. So I went out for fraternity rush, which for me was a little bold since I had no good clothes, no upper-class friends, and no money. My roommate was a guy named Jim Hersha. His background was similar to mine and, since misery loves company, we went through rush together. The first rush party we went to was at the Sigma Nu house. These people were nuts. They were the *Animal House* chapter. I swear to God, everything in that movie could have happened at Sigma Nu. When I was a junior, the alumni built them a huge beautiful new fraternity house. To get into the house when they had their big house-warming party, you had to throw a brick through one of the windows. Hersha and I decided that the Sigma Nus were a little too crazy, even for us.

We went to a few more parties before deciding that we were going to join the Kappa Sigs. Little did we know that we weren't supposed to be the ones deciding. This is how green I was: I walked down to the hall phone in Kincaid Hall, called the Kappa Sig house, and literally asked for the president of the chapter, Herschel Robinson. Herschel got on the phone, and I said, "Herschel? This is Jim Paul." Now Herschel Robinson didn't know Jim Paul or Jim Hersha from Adam's off ox. "My buddy Jim Hersha and I are going through rush and, frankly, we're a little tired of going to all these parties—the Delts, the Sigma Nus, the Sig Eps, the SAEs. We've kind of had it. We'd like to come over to the house and pick up our pledge pins." We went over to the house and, unbelievably, they gave us pledge pins. Now that I know how it is supposed to work, I can't believe we got away with that. We had the chutzpah to invite ourselves to be Kappa Sigs instead of their inviting us. We simply didn't know any better. We were breaking the rules and didn't even know it.

IS GIN A DRINK OR A CARD GAME?

When you join a fraternity, they make you do goofy stuff. It's a rite-of-passage thing. They make you shine shoes, clean windows, take out the garbage, just nickel-and-dime harassment stuff. One day I was at the house sitting on the floor shining shoes, and two actives, Johnny Cox and Pat Greer, were playing gin. In the middle of one of their games, Greer had to go somewhere. Johnny Cox looked over and said,

"Hey, pledge. Do you know anything about gin?"

"I know that if you drink as much of it as I did last night, your head hurts the next day."

"No, you idiot. The card game. Do you know how to play gin?"

"No sir, I don't. But I've always wanted to learn."

Now remember, I learned how to play cards at Summit Hills Country Club when I was ten years old. I'd been playing gin for eight years.

"Well, stop that shoe-shining shit, and come over here."

So, I went over to the table and he said, "All right, we're going to play gin. And understand, pledge, that you play gin for money."

"Yes sir, I understand that. But I don't have *any* money. I mean I *really* don't have any money."

The truth of the matter was, I didn't have any money. But I also wasn't that worried that I didn't have any money.

Cox said, "I understand that. I understand. We'll make it very, very cheap. You still have to play for money, but we won't play for any real money. We'll only play for five cents a point."

If you don't know anything about playing gin, you wouldn't know that five cents a point is real money. A nickel a point, a dollar a box, five dollars a game means you're probably playing somewhere in the neighborhood of ten to fifteen dollars a game. That isn't cheap. A game to 150 points might take 10 hands, 15 hands tops. Somebody's going to get to 150 about every twenty or thirty minutes. So now you're playing at a rate of about thirty dollars an hour. Now that is *real money*.

Cox explained the rules and told me how the score is kept and so on. Then he dealt out the cards. I would gin, and I'd ask, "I'm sorry sir, I've forgotten. What do I do again when I don't have a discard? When they all match?" And he'd go crazy. "Just lay 'em down pledge. Okay. Okay. You win." He really didn't think I knew a thing about what was going on.

We played for seventeen hours before he said, "That's it! I quit!" I won $612, which in 1962 was a whole lot of money. Tuition was $81 a semester, so $612 was big money. He didn't have $612 but he gave me $50 and owed me the rest. For the remainder of my pledge year I didn't have to shine any more shoes, clean garbage cans, or anything. He'd get other pledges to shine the shoes, and then I would credit him twenty-five cents a pair. Whenever the other actives wanted me to do something, I'd say, "Fine, write it down. Johnny, I'm supposed to clean the garbage cans. What do you think that's worth? Two dollars?

Okay, fine, subtract two dollars." Somebody else would have to do the garbage cans and I'd sit in there and play gin with Cox. That was another lesson in working smart instead of working hard.

Not having to do any more grunt work as a pledge sort of set me apart from the other pledges. I was also beginning to think of myself as a little different from most people; I succeeded at just about anything I did. I had followed the rules of the game in freshman English and succeeded. Then I had unknowingly broken the rules for entering a fraternity but still succeeded. I was a little different.

VERY LITTLE CLASS

I was beginning to think of myself as a little better than other people. I had a whole semester when I didn't even buy a book and rarely went to class. I'd get up around ten a.m. and go to The Grille in the Student Union building. That's where everybody went between classes. I'd sit and socialize, play hearts (another card game), talk to the women, make dates, and read the *Kentucky Colonel*, the school newspaper.

We not only met girls and made dates at The Grille, some of us met our wives-to-be there. I broke the rules and still succeeded in that arena, too. When I met Pat, I was dating two other girls, Sandra and Debbie, on a regular basis. I had just finished reading *Tortilla Flat* by John Steinbeck. The main character in the book is a guy named Danny. He and his friends are poor and lived up in the hills outside of Monterey, California. One of the themes of the book is that people can rationalize anything. For example, when a friend comes into some money, Danny steals it and rationalizes that he's actually doing the friend a favor by stealing it. "If I don't take the money away from my friend, he is going to use it to buy some wine, get drunk and maybe even burn his house down. It's just awful that he has this money. To be his friend, I need to steal the money from him and save him from himself."

I liked this book so much that I bought three more copies and gave one to Pat, one to Sandra, and one to Debbie. That was a mistake—a big mistake. Even though they were in different sororities, they used to meet in The Grille with a few other girls and have lunch. And one fateful day, all three girls were sitting there with the same damn book: "Gee, it's interesting you're reading that book." "Yeah, the guy I'm going with gave it to me." "Oh, really?" "Me, too." "Me, too." "Who might that be?" Little did I know that when it came to dealing with women, you shouldn't use the same modus operandi if you are going to go out with more than one of them at the same time. Why? Because women talk to one another, and if they find out you're treating each of them the same way, none will feel special and all of them will dump you. Luckily for me, Pat didn't dump me.

I just had this knack for doing things the "wrong" way but still succeeding. My first fraternity roommate was a guy by the name of Jim Dillon. He skipped a lot of classes, too, but he flunked out. Almost anybody who ran around with me flunked out. Hersha flunked out. Dillon flunked out. Dirken flunked out. A lot of people flunked out. But I didn't flunk out. This just reinforced my view that I was a little different and somehow a little better than everyone else. A few other guys tried to live with Dillon and me, but nobody could handle it. The reason they couldn't live with us is that we didn't do what students are supposed to do: go to school. We'd stay up all night, drink beer, and talk. After we took our dates home we'd get back to the room around eleven p.m. and then we'd sit and talk and drink beer until early in the morning. Well, you can't really stay up until three a.m. and make an eight a.m. class. So we didn't go to class very often.

Teachers don't like it when you don't go to class. And if you don't ever go, sooner or later you're going to have a problem. The first semester I lived in the fraternity house I ended up making every grade Kentucky had: A, B, C, D, E (E was an F at Kentucky), W (withdraw), and I (incomplete). I got them all.

Even though I rarely went to economics class, I made an A in the course. I understood it. The professor would talk about marginal propensity to consume and I'd say to myself, "I get it. That's a concept I can understand." I could look at those supply and demand curves and say, "Yeah, okay, I understand that. That makes sense. Okay, we're going to move supply here . . . yep, price will go down . . . yep, I understand." I didn't even own an economics book. I literally borrowed a book the night before the economics final, sat down and read the whole book for the first time. I went in and made an A because I understood it. I can remember taking the test thinking, "Okay, that question . . . he's talking about marginal . . . I can see it . . . okay, the chart looks like this . . . it's on the left side of the page . . . it should be somewhere around page 250, and what does it say?" I could remember exactly where it was, what it looked like, and what it said, and then I just wrote it down. I'm not claiming to have a photographic memory, but for that class I did. The professor hated it because I rarely went to class and I always made As on his tests. It really ticked him off. I wasn't doing what I was supposed to be doing, but I still did well in school.

I made the B in history and the C, D, and E in I can't remember what, and I made the W in philosophy. W is withdraw from the class with no grade, and it's beautiful because you don't get a bad grade. It's like you didn't even sign up for the course. God only knows why I signed up for philosophy. I hated it! It made no sense to me at all. It was all leftfield stuff: "I think, therefore I am." Who cares? It was like baseball to me: not very practical, so I had no problem withdrawing from philosophy.

A GLIMPSE OF THE FUTURE(S)

My incomplete course that semester was statistics. Although I liked the professor, Dr. Christian, I didn't like statistics; it was too hard. One day Doc Christian called me and said, "There's a friend of mine over here that you need to meet. I think you'd like what he does for a living. You're suited for this game." The old friend was Horace "Jack" Salmon, a UK graduate and the sales manager of a regional commodity-futures specialty brokerage firm in Louisville, Kentucky.

I didn't expect to know what he was talking about. I didn't know futures from past participles, but I respected Dr. Christian and thought, "Who knows? Maybe I'll like what Jack Salmon does for a living." So I went over to Christian's office to meet Salmon. Jack sat there and talked about soybean prices going up and going down, weather, Japan, acreage, yields, the excitement of the markets, and how you either make a lot of money or you lose a lot. The money thing got my attention.

"You can make money doing this?"

"You can make a lot of money."

Oops! That's what I wanted to do: make a lot of money. When people asked me what I was going to do when I got out of school, my answer was, "Make a lot of money." "Well, what are you going to do?" "I'm going to be in business." I didn't know how I was going to do it. I never thought about what I was going to do; it wasn't what you did for a living, it was how much you got paid for it.

OUT OF SCHOOL

I finally graduated in August 1965. Yes, August. I had to go to summer school to pass second semester freshman accounting. I hated accounting. Accounting to me was "find the missing nickel" bullshit. My attitude was: "I don't care where the nickel is. Pay someone to find it. Better yet, I'll give you a nickel. Just stop asking me to find the one that's missing." In August 1965 the war in Southeast Asia was rolling. I had signed up for ROTC in 1961 when I was a freshman and Vietnam was just starting. I figured that if it grew, I'd rather go as an officer than as a grunt. I had tried grunt and didn't like it. Officer was better. Officer was like a member of the country club; grunt was the guy who carried the bag. I knew I'd rather be the one telling the guy where to put the mortar than the guy carrying the mortar, so I signed up for air force ROTC. Then a friend told me that I could always go to Officer's Candidate School (OCS) once I had my college degree. Why should I do four years of this Mickey Mouse ROTC stuff when I could do six months of OCS later, and only if I had to? So I quit ROTC. That was a mistake—big mistake. True, OCS was only six months, but there were four more months of intensive training before you got in. And those ten months made ROTC look like a picnic.

After graduation I went on a couple of interviews but couldn't get a job offer. I was so 1-A nobody would hire me. (1-A was the draft board's term for being prime draft material.) It was obvious the only job offer I was going to get was to serve my country. There was nothing wrong with me; I wasn't flat-footed, I had 20/20 vision, and I wasn't married. The draft was in full force, and this was after the lottery so they were taking everybody. If you were 1-A, you were going— unless you came up with something really tricky.

Since I couldn't get a real job, I had to move back in with my parents and try to get a part-time job while I dealt with getting into OCS. I went down to the White Horse, a very nice dinner club where I had worked when I was in high school. I introduced myself to the owner, which was kind of audacious for a former bus boy. But, once again, I didn't know any better. I said to the owner, "Okay, here's my problem. I'm going to go into the military sooner or later, but in the meantime I'd like a job. I don't want to be a bus boy. I'm twenty-two years old and a college graduate, so I don't want to be a bus boy. I really don't want to be a waiter either. I think I'd like to be a bartender." To my surprise he said, "Okay."

I promise you, there is another society out there in America that is asleep right now. This society is made up of the "night people." It's people who work as waiters, waitresses, and all the other people that serve the entertainment and restaurant industry. They don't live in the daytime; they live at night. Within the night people's society, a bartender is very high on the totem pole. It's the same as being a doctor or a lawyer with day people. With night people, the head bartender at the right restaurant is right up there near the top. Within the night people's society, the head bartender at the Waldorf-Astoria in New York is a dude. All the waitresses, waiters, and bus boys think he's neat. The only guy cooler than the head bartender is the maitre d'. So if you're the number-two bartender, you're not far off the top. This was like being a Charlie Robkey among the night people. All of a sudden I found myself, at the ripe old age of twenty-two, very high up in the night people's society. I had thirty-year old waitresses who thought I was cute, and when they found out that I was going away to war, "Ohhhhhh."

YOU'RE IN THE ARMY NOW

Meanwhile I was having a problem getting into OCS, and the draft board was closing in. Why the problem? Well, because I had two misdemeanors on my record, both of which were related to spring breaks in Florida. One misdemeanor was for using a hotel's wooden deck chairs as firewood for a bonfire on the beach in Daytona. (It seemed like a good idea at the time.) The other was for breaking into an outdoor display case in Ft. Lauderdale to try to steal a mounted sailfish to take back to the frat house. (I can't even recall if that seemed like a good idea at the time.)

So when I tried to get into OCS and a question on the application form asked: "Have you ever been arrested?" I had to put "Yes." To get into OCS, I had to go to Washington. My father knew a federal judge and Pat's father was best friends with a congressman from Tennessee. So I went to Washington and met with the judge and the congressman. The federal judge was nice to put on the application, but it was the congressman who got the job done. This is when I learned that having hooks works. Knowing the right person to get something done will get it done. He said to me, "You sure you don't want to be in the navy? The navy owes me big. I could do the navy real easy." (The deal was: in the army's college-option OCS, when you graduated and got commissioned, you only had to serve two years. The navy was three; the air force was four. I was very interested in doing this in as short a time as possible.) I said, "No sir, I really want to be in the army." The congressman just picked up the phone, called the army, and bingo—I got in the army OCS. Now that's what I call having hooks.

Basic training and OCS are a lot like the pledge games in the fraternity. They test you by giving you things to do in impossibly short time frames. They do it to see what happens to you when you get stressed out. That's the game: "Let's give this guy an impossible situation and see what happens." It's like weeding out students with freshman English. If you don't know it's a game and how to play it, you will stress out. Their game plan is to get as many people as possible to quit in as short a time as possible. If you're focusing on this thing like it's really serious, then the training is very stressful. If you're focusing on it like: "This is a game and all these clowns are doing is trying to drive me crazy," it isn't hard. I had no problem with it. It was difficult in the sense that it was physically demanding, but it wasn't hard psychologically. I knew it was a game, and I understood their rules and their motivation.

The top 20 percent in the class were invited to stay at Aberdeen Proving Ground, Maryland, to be instructors for the new Ordinance OCS Program. Being an instructor is a great way to learn public speaking because you're in front of a bunch of officer candidates who have to be there and you outrank them. You don't have to be worried that they're going be unhappy with the job you're doing. You're the lieutenant, and they're the candidates. You're in total control. So if they make one wrong move, you shoot them. Since then I've spoken to audiences of fifty or more people more than a hundred times, and I love it.

After I graduated from OCS and became an OCS instructor, I had to go through Military Occupational Specialty (MOS) school. The first day of MOS school, a general came in and talked about the course. Then he said that at the end of the course they would recognize an honor graduate based on the highest academic standing and the highest this and the highest that.

I went home that night and said to Pat (we were married by then), "This is it! Everybody has been giving me this B.S. all my life that I don't do what I ought to do and I don't work to potential. All right, I tell you what I'm gonna do. I'm gonna be the damn honor graduate. I'm gonna be that man. I'm gonna do it. I'm gonna do whatever it takes to be that guy." At the end of the course I was the honor graduate. I couldn't believe it! I had done it, and it wasn't even that hard! All I did was figure out what the rules of the game were and then followed them.

Naturally, I had accepted the army's offer to be an instructor at Aberdeen. It was great! I became well known within the ranks as being a very good instructor. I was good at it. It's very easy to be an instructor when you say the same thing every week and they change the people you're saying it to. There's a lot of stuff I can't do, like math and statistics. But when He was passing out talents, He said, "And this one gets the gift of gab."

I was the first lieutenant at Aberdeen to become a master instructor. It was just another game to me. You had to do a bunch of B.S., and I did it. It wasn't hard. Every other master instructor had been at least a captain, and most were majors or lieutenant colonels. I was only a second lieutenant, the lowest ranking officer there is.

The master instructor title, OCS training, and the MOS honor graduate were the same deal: "It's a game. They wrote these rules; I understand these rules. I can follow these rules and win the game. It's no big deal. It isn't hard." Some of it was aggravating, but I didn't take it personally. There was nothing personal about it. They didn't know I existed when they wrote the rules so it was totally impersonal. You can either play the system or you can let the system play you. Pick one. I like playing the system because it's more fun and you win more. If you let the system play you, you can get very frustrated and very beat up.

After thirteen months at Aberdeen, I received orders sending me to South Korea. My record was starting to build. I'd just gotten the medal for the job I did as an instructor and the master instructor honor. The army is very big on that stuff so I got promoted to first lieutenant. They made me the adjutant, the guy in charge of personnel, for a battalion. I was the S-1 of the battalion at Camp Humphries, Korea. It was all paperwork. I had to sign everything. I hated paperwork, but I did it. I also did the rest of my job with a little more flair than my predecessors. I came up with ideas and new ways of doing things. I become noticed. I was not very good at being invisible.

One day I got a call from the XO (the number-two man) of the brigade, the unit above the battalion. He wanted to meet me for lunch. I cleared it with my boss (the military is very big on chain-of-command stuff) and met him for lunch. He offered me the job of S-3, which was the operations officer of the brigade. Now, understand that this was the equivalent of number-three man in the brigade. The organizational chart is: the brigade commander, then the brigade XO, then the S-3.

I was about five steps away from that S-3 position as the adjutant of the battalion so this guy wanted to multi-promote me five steps. The S-3 was usually a lieutenant colonel and I was only a first lieutenant! Realistically, I should have to go through captain, then major, then lieutenant colonel before I'd even be considered for this job. I became S-3 of the brigade at the ripe old age of twenty-three. I had about as much business being an S-3 as I did being a goalie on the Hartford Whalers. I didn't have any idea what I was doing. I was in way over my head; six-foot-three in ten feet of water.

One of the missions of this brigade was Eighth Army nuclear weapons storage. I had a sidearm—Top Secret this, Top Secret that. "Aye yi yi. I'm twenty-three years old! What am I doing? Are these people nuts? I don't need this responsibility. Jesus Christ! This is scary. My only claim to fame is that I was a master instructor back in Aberdeen, and that was easy. Two years ago I was burning hotel deck chairs for a bonfire on a beach in Daytona, Florida, and now I'm sitting on World War III! I'm nervous about this!" Someone else should have been doing this nuclear-weapons thing.

Since Vietnam was heating up so much during the 1960s, Korea was kind of in the background—until the *Pueblo* incident. In 1968 the North Koreans captured the intelligence ship U.S.S. *Pueblo* in international waters. The world would have been real scared if it had known that I had the position I had during the *Pueblo* affair.

My experience in the military reinforced my view that it really was money that was important in life, not what you did to make it. In the military it's the other way around. Your job is more important than money. Sure, I was S-3 as a first lieutenant instead of a lieutenant colonel, but I wasn't getting a lieutenant colonel's pay. I was only too happy to return to the real world again where money was what counted.

My mother had gotten me into Xavier University in Cincinnati on probation as a student in their MBA program. I was on probation because I only had a 2.2 grade-point average coming out of undergraduate school. Pat and I moved to Cincinnati and got an apartment. She started teaching, and I started school.

Because of my experiences in the army and especially because of what I had proved to myself by being the honor graduate, I wanted to do well in school this time around. I decided As were better than Cs. Fortunately, most of the classes I was taking were easy for me: marketing and economics, and no statistics or math. I don't like math. I can do arithmetic as well as anybody, but arithmetic and math aren't the same thing. I don't like formulas. If you put an x and a y on a page I go, "I don't care! Hire somebody to do that."

I cruised through the first-semester classes. Most of the other people in the program were General Electric engineers coming back to school to get their MBAs. There was a big GE plant outside Cincinnati in Evandale, and these guys were all either chemical or electrical engineers. They all carried slide rules on their belts (this was during the dark ages before hand-held calculators), but most couldn't spell marketing or economics.

Then we had to take a course called Quantitative Business Methods. It was a math course. The first day of class, this geek math teacher (who was a *total* math teacher: dull, dry, and two slide rules on his belt) started out by saying, "To pass this class you will need a working knowledge of calculus." Oops! I hadn't taken calculus. I wasn't going to take calculus. I couldn't spell calculus. But I had to have this course to graduate. I sat through the first few classes, but I didn't understand any of it. All these geeks I'd been laughing at in all these other courses were doing fine. They understood everything he was talking about. They had their little slide rules out arguing over the third place decimal to the answer, and I couldn't even get the right handle. I studied for two days for the first test and still only made a thirty-eight; the lowest grade in the class—by a lot.

So I called a buddy of mine I had gone to high school with who majored in math at Notre Dame. "Ralph, I need a tutor. I mean, I'm in deep, deep shit here. I'll pay you. I've got to pass this course. I don't know what I'm doing. I need somebody who can talk to me and make sense out of this stuff." He agreed to help me. The game was: I didn't care if I knew any of it. He just had to get me to where I could pass this course. I studied my tail off. I still didn't know any of it, but I did pull a C in the course.

The point was: I was laughing at all those guys in all the other classes because they couldn't carry my jock strap in economics and marketing, and all of a sudden I couldn't carry their jock straps in math. That taught me that there are people for places, places for people. You can do some things and you can't do other things. Don't get all upset about the things you can't do. If you can't do something, pay someone else who can and don't worry about it.

THE BRAIN WATCHERS AND THE BUTTERFLY

Since my grand plan was to "go into business" and "make a lot of money," becoming a stockbroker seemed like the perfect job. It's really just a well respected sales job, but if you're good at it the pay is super. I decided to get acquainted with some prospective employers for when I finished the MBA. I went down to "the street" in Cincinnati, and I started going to all the brokerage offices: Bache, DuPont, Hornblower—some of the names don't even exist anymore. I was looking for a part-time job that would accommodate my school schedule. The deal I wanted was this: "I can work part-time ten a.m. to three p.m. I don't care what I do. I don't care what I get paid, if I get paid. But when I finish graduate school, I want to go into your training program and become a registered broker." At most of the big firms I was a round peg in their square hole; they wanted full-time or nothing. One major wire house was the exception.

I walked into this office on just the right day in 1968. One of the biggest brokers in the office was primarily a commodities broker, and I happened to walk in the day after his assistant had quit. This broker was producing $300,000 to $500,000 a year in gross commissions—in commodities—in 1968! He was a big hitter.

The office manager's secretary said, "You'll have to talk to the office manager, Mr. Fitzgerald." I went in to talk to Larry Fitzgerald and he said, "What do you know about commodities?" I didn't know anything, but I remembered a few of the buzz words from the meeting I had with Jack Salmon and Dr. Christian in college. I said, "I've always been interested in futures. I'm particularly interested in the soybeans…and meal…and oil. Trying to figure out how the weather is going to affect the crop." I used the buzz words I had heard Salmon use. Fitzgerald said, "Okay, you're hired—if Cohan wants you. Go out and meet Ed Cohan." Cohan was the big commodities broker. Fitzgerald introduced me to him, and after a very short interview Cohan said, "Okay, you're hired."

On my way out of the office, Fitzgerald's secretary told me to come back the next day to fill out an application and take a test. "Test? What kind of test?" I asked. She said it was called the Minnesota Study of Values Test. Without knowing it, she had just let me know that there was a game to be played. This time the game was a test. I didn't know anything about this test, but I planned to find out about it.

I went straight to a bookstore and found a book titled *The Brain Watchers* that had three chapters on the Minnesota Study of Values Test. I bought the book and read it that night so I'd be ready for the test the next day. The questions on the MSV Test have five multiple-choice answers that you rank in their order of importance to you. The five categories of answers are Money, Politics, Aesthetics, Religion, and Social Significance. For example, one question I remember was:

When you look at Leonardo Da Vinci's painting *The Last Supper*, what do you feel? Rank the following in their order of importance, 1 being the most important and 5 being the least important.

The social implications of the event,
The beauty of the painting,
The value of the painting,

The political impact of the painting,
The religious ramifications of the painting.

Depending on what kind of job you are applying for, there is a right way and a wrong way to rank the answers. If you want to be a broker, the ranking for the question above is as follows: the highest ranking is the money answer, followed by the politics answer, social significance, aesthetics, and finally the religion answer. If you want to go to work as a parish priest, every right first answer is the religion answer, then social, and so on, and the money answer is always last. Once you know that's how their game is played, the test isn't hard. It's very simple. You can see very quickly which one of the five choices represents each of the categories; then you just rank them the way you believe the employer wants them ranked.

So the next day, I took the test and gave them 1, 2, 3, 4, 5 money, politics, social significance, aesthetics, religion on every question. I didn't even miss one on purpose to make it look good. That was a small mistake. I should have reversed 1 and 2 a couple of times, but I didn't. My test was perfect—absolutely no wrong answers. Now, when they grade this test, it comes out on a scattergram chart. If you're meant to be a broker, your scattergram looks something like a butterfly. Well, mine came out a perfect butterfly. Fitzgerald didn't care; he was going to hire me unless I really blew the test. But he did say, "You really did well on that test. I haven't seen anybody do that well before." I told him I had studied a little bit before I took the test. "You're not really able to study for that test."

"Well, you are, and you aren't," I said. The next day I started working as Cohan's assistant.

It was 1968, and the stock market was booming. It was going straight up, and everything was wonderful. Everyone in the office was making money. Then suddenly it stopped going up, and it started going down. When that happened, the only guy in the office making money was Ed Cohan. He was still doing business, and everyone else was looking at their phones. I said to myself, "Self,

I think I'm going into futures. I like the idea that I'm not at the mercy of the market only going up; I like the idea of being able to make money when the market goes down, too." I don't care how good a stockbroker you are; if the market is going down you're in trouble. You've got to take a defensive posture, and you're not going to do as much business.

I finished the MBA program in September 1969, and, as part of the deal I made with the brokerage firm, I was off to the three-month broker-training program in New York. I went to the Big Apple a month before the program started and spent that time in the futures division rubbing elbows with all the biggies. I wanted to know how they did what they did and why, what worked and what didn't work. I was on a fast track because I'd been working for Ed Cohan for a year, so everyone in the futures division in New York knew who I was. I was the one with the perfect butterfly chart.

Once again, I got the impression I was better than the others. I was "more equal" than the other trainees because I knew most of the people in the futures division and I worked for Cohan. Once we got into the actual training program, I ended up teaching part of the commodity portion of the program. The regular instructors were from New York, and they sort of knew what to say as far as the tests were concerned. But they didn't really know futures because the big futures exchanges were in Chicago. They quickly figured out that I did know what was going on, and they made me an assistant instructor. When they had questions on commodities, they would come to me. If I didn't know the answer, I knew I could get the answer from Cohan. Once again, I had the Midas touch and a hook.

Someone on the staff told somebody back in the futures division that I'd been a very big help teaching the class, and I got a call from Tom O'Hare, the firm's tax-straddle expert. He did huge production, $2 million or $3 million a year, all on referrals from stockbrokers. A broker would call and say, "I've got a client who's made $2.5 million this year. Can you do a tax trick?" Tom would say, "Yeah. How big a trick do you want? How much of that is he willing to risk to try to do it?" Tom O'Hare was a master at it.

Well, Tom called me and wanted to see me in his office. When I got there, we exchanged pleasantries, and then he pulled out my file. He said, "I really wanted to meet the prima donna who actually had the gall to paint a perfect butterfly."

"I'm sorry sir? I don't know what you're talking about."

"Yes, you do! Nobody could do a perfect butterfly unless he knew exactly what I'm talking about."

"Well, I read a book—"

"That book wouldn't be *The Brain Watchers* would it?"

"Well, let me see, as I recall . . . yes, I think that was the name of the book . . . and it helped me a lot on the test."

He said, "Okay. How close do you think you would really have come to the butterfly if you hadn't read the book?"

"To be honest, pretty close. If I hadn't known the game, I still wouldn't have been far off." (I wanted to be part of the country-club set, remember? I already believed money was important.)

"Okay. This is what I do."

Then O'Hare proceeded to tell me about tax straddles. The entire firm sent him referrals who were willing to risk some capital to reduce their tax liability legally. O'Hare needed an assistant. "I'm authorized to hire an assistant. I want someone who can learn what I do, understand what I do, and help me do what I do. That way we can do a lot more business. I've looked at your test—we both know *that's* B.S., but I give you credit for having done it. I've talked to your boss, Ed Cohan. He thinks you're a bright young man. I want you to come to work for me. I'll pay you $23,000 a year."

My alternative was to go back to Cincinnati as a broker under Cohan, basically as his assistant. But that wouldn't be bad. He was fifty-two years old, and he had a client book that was massive. He wasn't going to be there forever, so whoever went to work for him was going to inherit the book and make a lot of money. Back in Cincinnati I was probably going to make $15,000 to $18,000 plus whatever I could produce by getting my own customers. (At that time a $100,000 producer would have netted about $25,000—big money in 1968.) And this guy was offering me $23,000.

I said, "Mr. O'Hare, I'm extremely flattered that you called me in to see you. I think working with you would be absolutely super. But as flattered as I am, I don't think I can take the job."

Well, immediately it became obvious that this was not the kind of guy who was told "no" very often—particularly by some twenty-four-year-old who didn't know where the washroom was.

"What do you mean, you can't take the job?"

"Well, it's that number. I really don't want to live in New York, and neither does my wife. I could do it. I could open a travel agency in Kabul, Afghanistan, if the numbers were right. I have a new bride who's pregnant with our first child, and she doesn't want to move to New York. We could deal with it. But there would have to be some compensation for dealing with it, and, quite frankly, $23,000 doesn't do it."

"What do you mean? What are you going to make in your first year in Cincinnati?"

"Well, all I have to do is $100,000 in gross production and I'll make at least $25,000. Plus, you know Larry Fitzgerald is going to give me a bonus if I do $100,000 my first year. I'll probably make twenty-six or twenty-seven grand. So why would I want to come to New York for twenty-three grand when I know the odds are—"

"Wait a minute! You're going to do a hundred grand your first year?"

"Well, yeah, I think so."

"But aren't you going to be working for Cohan?"

"Yes sir, but he can't handle his book. His book is huge. I'll take what he can't get to. I think I can gross $150,000 out of his book in my spare time."

"Okay. I'll offer you $27,000."

"$30,000."

"Get out of my office."

"I went a little too far?"

"Yep. You went a little too far. Get out of my office."

"Mr. O'Hare, it's been a pleasure. I hope you have considered it a pleasure. I'll talk to you in a year, and we'll see who was right. I won't forget; please, don't you forget because, honest to God, I am flattered that you invited me in here and offered me the job."

I did $162,000 my first year; one of the highest production figures a rookie at the firm ever did. I called O'Hare and said, "I am LOS-2 [length of service, two years] as of today. Go over and check your little machine. You're going to find I did $162,000. I was right, and you knew I was right. Plus, Fitzgerald gave me a little kicker; I made 26.7 percent out of that $162,000. I made $43,000 in Cincinnati, which spends a lot better than $27,000 in New York. Would you like to reopen negotiations? I'm now $50,000 offer." He laughed and said, "No. I've gotten someone who may not have the chutzpah you do, but he'll do just fine for $28,000."

3

WOOD THAT I WOULD TRADE

Ayear after I started working for Cohan the firm decided to start something called regional trade units. The home office told us that if we were going to be in this region and do futures business, we had to be in Cleveland. I believed them. That was a mistake. I should have stayed with Ed Cohan. Unfortunately, he didn't tell me that was possible until it was too late. Cohan was the proverbial 500-pound canary; he could do whatever he wanted. If he had told the higher-ups that he wanted me to stay, I would have been able to stay. He was a great guy, but he wasn't aggressive. He didn't say, "Hey Jim, you don't have to do that. You can stay and work with me," so I figured I had to move to Cleveland.

I was flattered to be invited to interview for a job in the regional trade unit, considering that I was a twenty-four-year-old with only one year of experience. I was offered a position in Cleveland, and I took it. The deal was: all the stock brokers in the region would refer their futures business to two other futures brokers and me and take a split of the commissions. I moved to Cleveland in May 1970 and did a lot of business my first year, most of it in lumber. I developed a good client base and contacts in the lumber industry. One day our little group, which had grown to five from three, did more business in futures that all of the 112 stock brokers in the office did in securities, combined!

Between knowing Cohan, teaching in New York, and producing some of the firm's best LOS-1 figures ever, I was pretty full of myself. I continued to believe that I was different and better than the run-of-the-mill broker. Believing I could bend or break the rules led me to do something really stupid—not illegal, just a little ahead of its time and more than just a little against firm policy. One of my customers had a trading system, and he wanted to manage some outside money. He proposed that I raise $30,000 and put it into an account. He would trade the account, take no fees, and split profits *and* losses fifty-fifty with the customers who had put up the money. This sort of arrangement is done all the time today and usually under terms much less advantageous for the customer. Today there are usually fees, and no money manager shares in the losses.

So I raised the money and informed the customers exactly what we were doing, and they signed papers agreeing to the terms. I even documented the arrangement with the state securities authorities by registering the account as a limited partnership. But I opened the account as an individual account, which it really wasn't.

Well, the guy made money for a while, but then he started losing money. After he lost $20,000 of the customers' money, I started getting antsy and said, "Okay, no big deal, but you need to put up your half of those losses: $10,000." He sent a check. The check bounced. Naturally, that caught the attention of the operations manager. The long and short of it is that the trader lost the original $30,000 and $20,000 more. He couldn't, or wouldn't, pay the $20,000 owed to the firm, and I got fired. I was terminated "for cause," which is a big no-no as far as the New York Stock Exchange is concerned. I got blackballed. I couldn't get a job anywhere. Soon after that the firm collected the money from the client, but a fat lot of good it did me by then.

So I called my friend Jack Salmon, who by then was the president of the regional brokerage firm he was working for when I met him back in college. I hadn't had a job for three months, and I really didn't want to go to work for a regional firm. But you gotta do what you gotta do. I still had a client base that I thought I could move. "I'm sure I can move the lumber accounts. Do you know any firms where I could take my business?" I said.

"Come to work for us," he said. "My Cleveland office could really use your talents. I'll pay you 50 percent of gross. Plus I'll pay you a 5 percent override on the whole office." My previous employer had only paid me 25 percent of gross, so this was a great deal if I could continue to do the business. Sometimes, knowing the right people and being in the right place at the right time can make all the difference in the world. I went to work for Salmon in a tiny four-man office in Cleveland. Most of my accounts transferred over, so business was back to normal fairly quickly.

I made good money between January 1973 and July 1976. All the commodity markets got hot when Nixon took us off the gold standard in 1971, and the grain markets went crazy in 1973 and 1974. My clients were making money, and I was making money. I bought a house and a sports car. I went to the managers' meetings, and I was honored as the leading manager based on production improvement. Once again, I encountered the Midas-touch syndrome; everything I touched turned to gold. I didn't think things could get any better than that, but they did.

CHICAGO

The only commodity-exchange membership I had ever wanted was one that would enable me to trade lumber without having to pay for the right to trade all the other commodities, which came with a full membership. In 1976 the Chicago Mercantile Exchange created exactly that kind of membership. Leo Melamed, chairman of the CME at the time, came up with a brilliant gimmick to pay for the new Merc building by selling equity in the exchange without diluting the full memberships. He created a Non-Livestock Membership (NLM) that permitted you to trade lumber and eggs. The NLM seat cost $20,000 compared to the going rate of $125,000 to $150,000 for a full membership at the CME or the Chicago Board of Trade.

I called Jack Salmon and said, "This is it! I want to move to Chicago. There's really no one in the office here in Cleveland other than me anyway, so let's bag this thing and I'll move to Chicago." I bought the seat and moved to Chicago in June 1976.

I wanted to dress for success for my new job in Chicago. An old fraternity brother of mine, Jimmy Showalter, had a men's clothing store in Lexington, Kentucky. Jimmy's store had nice clothes: Hickey Freeman kind of stuff. Not Armani, but very nice. I called him and asked if I could come into his store on a Sunday when he was closed and deck myself out in a new wardrobe. "Well what are we talking about here, Jim?" he asked me. I could tell he didn't want to come in on a Sunday just for me. I said, "I'm talking about spending some serious money on new clothes. Maybe $8,000 or $10,000 to have it done right." Suddenly, Sunday didn't sound too bad to Jimmy. So I flew to Lexington and got a new wardrobe.

When you buy a seat on the exchange, you get to select the call letters that will be engraved on your ID badge that other traders use to identify you when they trade with you in the pit. You want to stand out in the crowd so traders will trade with you often. Some people use their initials, nickname, or some catchy combination of letters that makes them easy to remember. In my case, since I was always looking for whatever edge I could get, I picked the initials LUCK. I'd rather be lucky than good anyway. I thought by calling myself lucky maybe I'd be lucky; plus, it was very easy to remember. Everybody knew who LUCK was. It was a badge that people could instantly identify with and remember.

LEARNING THE TRADING FLOOR

Very quickly, it became obvious to me that the best trader in the lumber pit was a guy named Stu Gimble. He was head and shoulders above everybody. Just like at the country club when I wanted to ingratiate myself with the movers and shakers, I wanted to get to know Gimble. So, not knowing any better (just like when I got my pledge pin), I walked up to him one day and said, "Stu, can I take you to lunch?"

"I don't go to lunch."

"Can I take you to dinner? Can I take you for a drink? Look, you can call it anything you want, I just want to go out and talk with you. You're the best trader in the pit so you're the man I gotta talk to."

"Okay, we'll go to lunch."

Once again, I set myself apart from the rest of the crowd by getting to be friends with Stu Gimble and another phenomenal trader on the floor, Joe Siegel. Joe moved around mostly in the pork bellies and the lumber pits. I learned a lot from the two of them. I still think Gimble was the best mechanical trader ever on the floor.

LIFE IN THE FAST LANE

As part of this new Non-Livestock Membership the Board of Governors of the CME decided to have two new governors from the NLM Group on the board. There was a nominating committee to choose four people from the NLM Group to run for those two spots, and I was approached and asked if I'd be interested in running for the board. I guess I looked gubernatorial wearing these fancy-schmancy clothes to the floor. The dress code for the floor was a tie and your trading jacket—no jeans or tennis shoes. Everybody else was wearing khakis and corduroys and I was walking around in $600 vested suits. I'd have my trading jacket on over a vest and a $50 tie. I was well dressed for just about any business environment, but on the floor I was extremely well dressed. Once again, I thought I was a little different from, and a little better than, other people.

The idea of a contest for a Board of Governor's seat was flashing "game" to me. It was like freshman English, mind games in the military, and the MSV test. I said, "Sure, I'd love to be a candidate."

Now, what do you do when you're in high school and someone asks you to run for student council? You say, "Sure." But then you don't run; you anti-run. Everything is done to deemphasize it because you don't want the embarrassment of trying and losing. So I said to myself, "Self, whether you lose because you didn't run for the Board of Governors or whether you lose because you ran hard, it's the same outcome. So let's really run hard. Let's get aggressive and try to get elected. And if you don't get elected, you don't get elected. Big deal."

I did everything I could to get elected. I sent platform letters. I had Jack Salmon send letters. Then I sent hand-written letters asking for votes. Well, nobody else was really running. They were all doing the "I don't want to run because I don't want to lose" routine. If you run aggressively in that situation, you win by a landslide. I won 121 votes out of 150 votes.

I was elected to the Board of Governors of the CME after only six months in Chicago. I was thirty-three years old, looked like I was twenty-five, and acted like I was twenty-two, but I was on the Board of Governors. After the election, Leo Melamed came up to me and said that I would also represent the NLM on the Executive Committee of the Board of Governors since I had the most votes in the election. It turned out the Executive Committee was where everything really happened. Anytime you see a committee of more than ten, it isn't the real committee. There's a subcommittee somewhere making the decisions. So the board at that time was eighteen members and the Executive Committee was six. I couldn't believe I had just been elected to the Board of Governors, and I didn't even know the Executive Committee existed. But suddenly I was on it. I had only been in town six months, and I was elected because I had presence, wore a vest and $80 shoes, knew a lot about the markets, and knew a lot of people in the industry.

Through a series of chance occurrences, I became a player in the cradle of the futures industry. All of a sudden, I was in the inner circle. Fortunately, once I got there I wasn't bad at the game. I played by the rules and became very involved in the exchange and the industry. It was a very heady experience to be an exchange official after such a short time in Chicago and to be friends with the two best traders on the floor after such a short time in the pit. I began to think of myself as one of the "bigger players." I was going to the floor every day, and while most of my trading was still focused on customer business, I was starting to trade more for my own account. I was probably making $200,000 to $300,000 a year and spending a lot of it. I can't even remember half the stuff I bought. I also made investments that I can't even remember. My ego was getting fed from all quarters: I was a governor, a member of the Executive Committee, and friends with Gimble and Siegel. I was a little different. I was a little better than the rest of the crowd, just like getting my pledge pin in college and the multi-promotion in the military. I remember one morning I was heading out the door on my way to work, and I stopped at the mirror in the hall tree to straighten my tie. I looked at myself, and I said, "Goddamn. Life in the *fast* lane." Life was great, and I didn't think it could get any better. But it did.

ZENITH

There was another guy at my firm who was also involved in the lumber market. Larry Broderick had come from the cash lumber business and was working in our St. Louis office. Both of us were doing some business with Potlatch, a huge paper-manufacturing and lumber firm in the northwest. The Potlatch family had been cutting wood since Noah's flood, and the guy who ran their trading operation was a guy named Tom Tomjack. One day Tomjack called me and said, "This is stupid. We've got you doing your thing in Chicago and Broderick doing his thing from St. Louis. You guys ought to be working together. Why don't we all get together, have lunch, and talk about it?"

When we met him on the West Coast for lunch, he said, "Look guys, together you two would make the best single broker in the business. Why don't you figure out a way to work together and stop being two independents." So we did. We became partners, and very shortly we started doing a lot of business because the arrangement really worked. Larry had fantastic connections in the cash market, and I great floor information and execution services.

I was walking into the lumber pit every day with big orders. "Buy fifty of this. Sell one hundred of that." When you start doing size like that in the pit, it can really do to your head; the other people in the pit don't know whether the orders are for your account or for a client's. It also makes it very easy to start trading that kind of size for your own account. I was the biggest broker in the pit in terms of doing size orders. Larry and I had a large percentage share of the market. Lumber volume was something like 3,000 or 4,000 contracts a day and we were doing 600 or 800 contracts a day between client and personal trading. At six-foot-three with a booming voice and one-hundred-lot orders, I became a presence in the pit.

So not only did I think I was neat, but a lot of other people did, too. I thought I was different and somehow better than other people; like I had some sort of Midas touch. I might have thought it was true, but it wasn't. Little did I know that all the times I thought I was good, I had only been lucky. For example, when I was sent to Korea and became an S-3 as a second lieutenant, was it because I was good or lucky? Lucky. Everyone else was sent to Vietnam, so there was a personnel shortage in Korea. When I happened into that brokerage the day after Cohan's assistant quit, was it because I was good or lucky? Lucky. When I became a board governor and Executive Committee member after only six months in Chicago, was it because I was good or lucky? Lucky. The successes in my life had given me a false sense of omniscience and infallibility. The vast majority of the successes in my life were because I got lucky, not because I was particularly smart or better or different. I didn't know it at this point in the story, but I sure as hell was about to find out.

4

SPECTACULAR SPECULATOR

TIMBER TUMBLES

I will never forget the first day I made $5,000 trading. I felt exactly the same way I did the first day I made five dollars caddying when I was ten years old. To make the five bucks, I caddied all day long. I made five dollars for ten hours of carrying a golf bag. Fifty cents an hour. It was the greatest feeling in the world. Then there was the first day I made $10,000. Same feeling. Then the first day I made $20,000, and so on.

I remember one Thanksgiving I was at home in Kentucky with my folks and my brother. The Friday after Thanksgiving my brother and I flew to Chicago so he could see what I did for a living. I was long the lumber market and losing about $40,000 or $50,000 on this position when we arrived in Chicago. We went into the lumber pit and I explained how everything worked. Then to demonstrate how things worked, I bought ten contracts. The market went down and I bought some more. After a little while the market turned and roared to the upside and I bought it all the way up. We walked out of the pit with $37,000 in an hour of trading. It was just one of those days when the market was going to go up because I was buying it. Some days you just can't do anything wrong. Including all the money my customers made that day plus all the commissions I generated, we made about $100,000. And it felt just the same as the first day I made five dollars caddying.

In December 1980 Broderick and I were at the height of our business. We had accounts with everybody who was anybody in the lumber business, so we had a very impressive customer list and an equity run with over $3.5 million on it. We were approached by the new president of another regional firm. He was trying to turn it around and wanted us not only for our customer business but also for my stature in the industry. If I went with his firm, he would gain some immediate credibility that he was turning this little firm around. So he made us a deal that was just crazy: 50 percent payout, expense accounts, super-neat office, fancy furniture, built-in bar. I literally told him at the time that there was no way he was going to make any money on the deal, but he did it anyway. This was probably the zenith of my career. I was making plenty of money, I had good accounts, and I was on the Executive Committee and Board of Governors. Life was great.

With interest rates skyrocketing in 1979 and 1980, the housing market, and consequently the lumber market, felt the pinch. The high interest rates depressed new homes sales, the main market for lumber. Lumber prices plunged, and volume in the lumber pit dried up. It went from about 6,000 contracts a day down to 1,000. I don't care what your market share is; when the market shrinks by that amount, you've got problems. There was no longer enough business in lumber futures for me to maintain my lifestyle.

THE ARABIAN HORSE FIASCO

I figured I could apply my "money-making talents" to other business ventures and maintain my lifestyle. "I know what I'm doing. I'm smart, and I have the net worth to prove it." One of the smartest guys I ever met was Jim Gleasman. He was also one of the craziest people I ever met. He had this knack of being the big-picture guy. He was always coming up with grand schemes to make money. In one of his schemes, we were going to buy an island off the coast of South America. It cost something like $2 million. But we were going to leverage the purchase by putting down only $100,000 and borrowing the rest using the teakwood grown on the island as collateral. We were going to harvest the teakwood, sell it, make a fortune, and then own the island for nothing. Gleasman was nuts—he was constantly coming up with these ideas. Every week he'd have a new way to make a million dollars.

One day he started talking about Arabian horses. "You buy these beautiful horses and you breed them and you show them in horse shows and you make a lot of money."

"Are you sure that's right?"

"Yeah."

I never could get a handle on why or how you made a lot of money with these horses. These things don't *do* anything. They don't race or run the steeplechase—nothing. They're show horses. You walk them around and somebody pays $2 million for this thing that walks around looking pretty. Sounded crazy to me, but Gleasman and I started looking at Arabian horses.

He came up to me one day and said, "I've got it. I found a couple who are getting divorced, and they're selling everything they own in common to settle their divorce decree. They have an Arabian horse we can buy for $22,000." This was the first number he'd mentioned that I could even think about paying for a horse that didn't do anything. So we went and saw this horse. His name was Onyx. Onyx was beautiful. Gorgeous. A dark gray Arabian. He had this pedigree and that pedigree, and so on. "Okay, let's do it. Buy the horse. What's it gonna cost?"

The minute you buy one of these things, the cash register just starts running. We had to transport it over to the stables, pay for room and board, pay the vet, and pay for training. After a few months, it was getting to be kind of expensive. We had something like $20,000 each in Onyx.

Then one day I got a call from Gleasman.

"It's Onyx," he said.

"What do you mean, *it's Onyx?*"

"They just checked Onyx into the emergency room of the Ohio State equine hospital."

"Ah, God. Now what?"

"He's got a rare blood disease."

Naturally, we hadn't insured Onyx yet. We figured that after training him and documenting his pedigree, he was going to be worth more and we'd be able to insure him for a lot more. The SOB ran through another thirty grand before he died. The Arabian horse fiasco cost me about $50,000 before it was over. Here I was thinking I could make money in Arabian horses, and I couldn't even ride one.

SOYBEAN OIL SPREADS

I decided to stay away from horses and stick with the markets where at least I thought I understood what was going on. So as the lumber market dried up, my business changed. I gradually moved my business away from the floor and started handling more speculative customer business from upstairs, trading from a quote machine and doing more general futures business instead of just lumber. I started opening some speculative accounts and getting my lumber accounts interested in trading other markets, too.

With this change in my business, I needed some help. I knew a lot about the lumber market, but not too much about other markets. An old friend of mine, Kirby Smith, had also joined this regional firm. This was the old "pay someone who knows" routine. I knew Kirby from my days at the other regional firm, and we had kept in touch. I had always been impressed with the depth and breadth of his knowledge of the markets. He just knew stuff that I didn't know. It was a classic case of "anybody who knows more than I do must really be smart, because I know I'm pretty smart." Kirby was brilliant; he really knew what he was talking about in a lot of markets, particularly the grain market.

In the summer of 1982 Smith started focusing on the soybean market. The beans had been in a bear market since 1979. Kirby had this really big thing for soybean oil. (Soybean oil is made from crushing soybeans into oil and meal.) He was talking about how the supply of bean oil was getting tight, there would be a shortage, and the price was going to go straight up. Now, all I knew about soybean oil was that it was used to make mayonnaise, and as far as I could see there were plenty of jars of Hellmann's on the shelf at the grocery store. But, as I said, Kirby was brilliant. He knew all there was to know about this market. Pretty soon I began to learn a lot about it, too, and I started following the soybean market very closely.

In early 1983, we started building bull spread positions in bean oil. (We were bullish, so we were long the nearby month of soybean oil and short a deferred month. If there was a shortage and supplies got tight, the nearby month price would go up more than the deferred month, and we would make money.) As always, when I started to believe in something I really believed. I called everybody I knew and told them "our" story about soybean oil and told them to get involved so they could make some money. If you even thought you knew my name, you had bean-oil spreads on. I called everybody: my brother, traders, friends, customers. My secretary heard me tell the story on the phone so many times she even opened an account and put five spreads on for herself. The neat thing about these spreads was you didn't have to put up any initial margin. They were marked to the market at the close of each day so you had to cover any paper loss, but it didn't require any money to open a position. That enabled us to build up big positions. And I mean big positions. So big that one day the Chicago Board of Trade called to inform me I had exceeded the speculative position limit of 540 spreads. They made me sell out to the point where I was holding *only* 540 spreads. So not only did I have on 540 spreads, but there were another 700 spreads among all these other people to whom I had told "our" story.

ROAD TO RICHES

That summer Pat and I had planned to do something we had never done: take a real family vacation. We were going to take the kids and travel the upper East Coast. Things were going so well with business that before we left on the vacation, I went out and bought a brand-new Porsche 911 convertible. Then I went and spent $11,000 to rent a forty-five-foot motor home for the entire month of August.

The plan was to leave Chicago, go to Washington, D.C., to visit my brother, Terry, and then head up the East Coast. I had a phone installed in the motor home so I could keep up with the markets from the road. We left Chicago the first thing in the morning Monday, August 1, 1983. About lunchtime I called Smith from my mobile phone in the motor home.

"Hey. What's the soybean market doing today?"

"Beans are twenty cents higher."

"Great! Why are we up?"

"A weather report calling for unseasonably hot, dry weather for at least the next ten days."

I loved it. While I was on vacation, the soybean crop was going to roast in the worst drought since the Dust Bowl days of 1936–37. I was going to get paid by the market to be on vacation. I thought to myself, "Maybe we'll go all over the country next year and I'll just trade from on the road."

"What's the lumber market doing?"

"It's limit down."

"Ouch."

Well, I was up more in the bean oil that I was down in the lumber, so I was still up on the day.

We pulled into my brother's on Wednesday, August 3. The next night some of Terry's friends came over for dinner. They had just seen a new movie about the commodities markets called *Trading Places*, and they wanted to know all about the commodities markets and the life of a trader. So I stayed up half the night telling them war stories about my experiences in the markets. When they found out about the lumber position I had on that was just killing me, they couldn't believe I could have such a loss and handle it. I also told them about the killing I was making in the soybean-oil market. They were all caught up in the conversation because of the movie they had just seen.

The next day lumber was limit down. So I called Smith. "See if you can call somebody and find out why lumber is down so much." He came back with a story that some huge commodities fund was liquidating a large position to keep from taking delivery of lumber. "Well, okay," I thought to myself, "that's no big deal. The market will start back up after this clown gets out of the market." But the market continued limit down for three days. Limit down for three days on fifty or sixty contracts adds up to real money. I was down about $70,000. Finally, I started asking Smith some intelligent questions like: "What are the spreads doing? Where is the cash market trading? What is plywood doing?" The bull spreads had been deteriorating for about eight days or so, but that day they were starting to turn back around. "Okay. Buy twenty contracts at the market." With the market turning, I figured I would add on to the position so I could make back the money more quickly. Then we left Terry's and continued the vacation.

Well, it turned out the day I bought those last twenty contracts was the low in the market for a while and the market rallied $13.50 per thousand board feet in about a week. Somewhere around Philadelphia I had gotten about $50,000 of the $70,000 back. "Victory, out of the jaws of defeat," I thought to myself. I was driving down the Jersey Turnpike, drinking Budweiser, talking on the phone, trading commodities, and thinking I was the neatest guy in the world.

Fortunately, the lumber position didn't force any change in the real position—soybean oil. I'd call Smith a couple of times a day to see how the bean-oil market was doing.

"How's it look?"

"Oh, it looks great!"

"Yeah, I thought so."

"Yeah, we're fine."

"Yeah, I wish we could buy some more."

We would go back and forth like this with the old "buddy" routine, preaching to the converted. There's nothing worse than two people who have on the same position talking to each other about the position.

"How's it look?"

"Oh, it looks great. Beans are limit up and so is bean oil. This thing is bullish as hell."

"Are they still focusing on the weather?"

"Yeah, and also that Fed Chairman Volker and Treasury Secretary Regan have launched a coordinated intervention in the currency markets with European central banks to push down the value of the U.S. dollar."

"That'll help our exports and push grain prices up even more, won't it?"

"That's right."

After the close on August 11, the Agriculture Department released a crop report indicating damage to the crop as of an August 1 survey. The market had been up strong for several days going into the report. I called Smith.

"How's the market?"

"Limit down and our bull spreads in bean oil are losing some ground."

"Limit down? Why? I thought the report was bullish, didn't you?"

"Yeah, but hurricane Alicia has moved into the Gulf of Mexico, and the market thinks the rains from the storm will help the crop in the Mississippi Delta."

"That's the stupidest thing I ever heard. Alicia isn't going to spawn gentle spring showers. Those storms are going to be so violent they'll probably rip the soybeans right out of the ground. I think the market should be up." The market was limit down again the next day and the bull spreads in oil lost some more ground.

One of the oldest rules of trading is: If a market is hit with very bullish news and instead of going up, the market goes down, get out if you're long. An unexpected and opposite reaction means there is something seriously wrong with the position. Two consecutive limit down days following the release of a supposedly bullish government report does not indicate a strong market. Faced with that situation, what did these two bold and committed traders do? Get out or confidently hold onto their position and opinion? That's right! We decided the market was wrong, and we were not going to let *them* get us out of this great position. Within days the market turned and was moving our way again. Break the rules, maintain your conviction, and reap the rewards. Our courage under fire was about to be rewarded.

The evening of Wednesday, August 24, we pulled into Larry Broderick's lake house just outside of Cleveland. We were wrapping up the vacation, and I wanted to be back in the office the following Monday. Larry and I got up the next morning, went into his office in the house, made some phone calls, watched the markets a little bit, and then went out onto the dock. At the end of the dock he had a quote machine, a phone, and a little refrigerator. We were sitting out in the sun on the last Thursday in August 1983, watching our market positions, drinking a beer, and thinking life couldn't get any better. But it did.

Monday, Tuesday, and Wednesday of that week the bean-oil market had closed limit up, so the spreads hadn't made or lost any money for us. But on Thursday the spreads started to trade. The September bean oil that we were long went up 150 points, and the January month that we were short went up only 80 points. The contracts further out closed lower on the day. The bull spreads were working like a charm. At the end of the day, I had made $248,000. In one day—a quarter of a million dollars!

Now, remember that all the people I knew in the whole world had these bean-oil spreads on. My secretary made $2,400 that day. (That's real money when you're making $35,000 a year.) Broderick made almost $50,000. Including all the people I had told about this bean-oil trade we were up almost $700,000 in one day. I was getting calls from all over the country telling me how great this was and how smart I was. And I agreed, "Yes, I am so smart. But this is just the beginning. This bean-oil market has a long way to go, and we are all going to get rich."

I also heard through our contacts in the market (since now we were pretty big players in the bean-oil market) that it looked like the primary guy on the other side of this trade from us was none other than the legendary trader Richard Dennis. (Richard Dennis, dubbed the "Prince of the Pit," borrowed $1,600 from his family in 1970, bought a seat at the minor-league Mid-America Commodity Exchange for $1,200, and ran the remaining $400 into a reported $200,000,000 over the next fifteen years.) "Ohhhh," I said. "That's good news. We're gonna take out Richard Dennis. We'll go down in trading history as the guys who took out Rich Dennis. Can you stand it?" Not only were we going to be rich, we were going to be famous, too.

THE DEATH-KNELL PHONE CALL

The high from "being right" the market and making all that money is unbelievable. It cannot be duplicated with drugs. You are totally invincible. You are impervious to all pain. There's nothing bad in the world. It's literally like you expect God to call any minute and ask, "Is it okay if I let the sun come up tomorrow morning?" And after thinking about it for a minute you'll probably say, "Yeah, go ahead." I called Smith and we mutually congratulated each other on our wisdom and knowledge and for all the money we were now going to make—not the money we had made but the money we were *going* to make. We immediately accepted the money we had made and assumed that it was in our bank accounts. It was ours. We weren't even saying, "Isn't it neat that we made an unconscionable amount of money today?" That was a given. We were talking about all the money we were going to make. That day simply confirmed that we were right. I'll never forget going into Larry's house that afternoon and picking up a copy of *The Robb Report*. Originally a magazine that listed used Rolls Royces for sale, it grew into the magazine to list ridiculously expensive things for sale: real estate for $5,000,000 and up, hunting lodges, estates, whole islands for sale. Everything in this magazine was the most expensive of its kind. If it were selling pens, they'd be priced at $500 each.

There was a section on motor homes, and the Rolls Royce of motor homes was a thing called a Blue Bird Wanderlodge. I was sitting in the house, looking through *The Robb Report*, and honestly thinking about buying a $400,000 motor home. Why would anyone spend a half a million dollars for a bus? You'd have to be nuts. I was nuts! I was really thinking about buying this bus.

Friday morning I got up, went straight to the quote machine, and sat on the edge of my seat moments before the market opened, saying, "Come on guys, open this sucker. Let's get going. I want to make some more money." I literally assumed I was going to make more money. The question was not *whether* I was going to make money. The question was *how much* money was I going to make. There was a total presumption of success; what had gone before would continue.

The market opened and the spreads corrected about ten points or so from the previous day's huge rally. But that was $30,000 on my position! "No big deal," I thought to myself. (Here's another sign of having lost control. Here's someone who has lost $30,000 and is saying, "Hmmm. That's not so bad." That's a little nuts. Right? I'd just lost $30,000 in the first five minutes of Friday and I was feeling fine. "No problem. Too bad we can't buy more of these.")

The market came back during the day from down ten to up thirty points, and did it right on the close. Bang! The spreads went our way again. Perfect! You couldn't have written the script any better. Now we had Richard Dennis trapped over the weekend—or at least we thought we did. We actually had the chutzpah to think it was "good news" that wonder-trader Richard Dennis was on the other side of our position.

I made $60,000 that day. But the best part of it was that the market moved perfectly. In the last five minutes of trading the front month rallied sharply. I made $60,000, which meant another $150,000 or so was made by the group. The clients were calling again, "Ah, God, this is wonderful. You guys are so smart." Naturally, I agreed with them.

On Saturday my family and I drove back to Chicago. When I returned the motor home, I just turned it in and paid them another $500 or $1,000, whatever it was, to take care of the phone, etc. I just didn't want to bother with stuff. I was above all of that. My attitude was: "How much money does it take to make whatever I want to happen, happen? Fine. Do it. Here's the money."

SOYBEAN OIL GETS SLIPPERY

Monday morning I got in my brand new Porsche 911 convertible, put the top down, and took the outer drive by Lake Michigan to downtown Chicago. I got into the office at about seven-thirty, a full two hours before the bean market opened. The sofa and chair in my office were covered in some special leather from West Germany. I think the set cost $7,000. The stereo was a $4,000 Bang and Olufsen. Everything in this office was about the most expensive you could make it. It was like *The Robb Report*: "How much can you spend on a desk? Fine. I'll buy it." I had a special desk that was on a copper pedestal coming out from the floor and the carpeting covered the base of it. On top of the pedestal was a giant 3′ x 6′ x 7″ piece of mahogany. The tabletop looked like it was suspended in midair. The credenza didn't touch the floor either. It was a matching piece of wood bolted to the wall, also looking like it was suspended. When you walked into the office all you could see was carpet stretching out in front of you, a copper column rising up from the carpet, and two pieces of wood levitating in midair, defying gravity. And that is just what I thought I was doing: defying gravity. I sat down at my fancy desk on the edge of my chair waiting for the market to open, ready to have another $50,000 day, and thinking life couldn't get any better than this. This time, I was right. It didn't.

When the bean-oil market opened that Monday morning, the spreads opened a little against us. By the close of trading, the bean-oil spreads had given back most of the gains of the previous two days because of rain in the soybean belt over the weekend. I figured it was no big deal since the market had been up so much in recent weeks. "It's just a correction in a continuing bull market," I told myself. "Besides, it is too late in the growing season for rain to do the crop any good."

On Wednesday, August 31, the oil spreads got smashed again, despite the fact that soybeans were twenty-five cents higher on rumors the Soviets were negotiating agreements to buy soybeans from the United States. I was sure that with the beans up so much and the Soviet news, it was just a matter of time before the oil market caught up.

On Thursday the whole soybean complex (beans, meal, and oil) collapsed on reports a Soviet jet fighter shot down a Korean Air Lines passenger plane.

"What does the KAL downing have to do with the bean market?" I asked.

"They think we'll impose a grain embargo against the Soviets just like Carter did when the Russians invaded Afghanistan in 1980," said Smith.

"That's stupid. The Russians didn't invade Korea. They accidentally shot down a passenger plane. There's no comparison. The market's wrong; we're not going to have a grain embargo."

I was right. Over the Labor Day weekend President Reagan condemned the Soviet assault but shunned tough retaliation. He refused to disrupt a new grain sales accord. Soybeans rallied sharply on the news, but the bull spreads in the oil market went down again. Once again, I chalked it up to the fact that the oil market had outperformed the beans in August; the beans were playing catch up, and the oil market was resting before the next leg up. The spreads did stabilize for a couple of days as the market began to focus on the September 12 release of the Agriculture Department's crop report. That report turned out to be wildly bullish: the damage to the crop was more severe than previously thought. Beans opened almost limit up the next day, but closed almost limit down. However, the bull spreads in oil closed higher on the day.

"Okay," I said to myself, "this oil market is starting to turn back to the upside. This whole bull market was driven by the oil market, and bean oil is starting to rally again. This market is turning." But the next day the oil market collapsed again. Limit down in all contract months and more than limit down in the spot month since there were no limits on the spot month.

On Friday the market stabilized and managed to erase about a third of the week's losses. On Monday, September 19, the bean market and the oil market roared to the upside. Over the weekend a winter storm system in Canada exploded and was drifting toward the Midwest. "This is great," I thought to myself, "just a few weeks after the worst drought since the 1930s wreaked havoc with most of the soybean crop, an early frost threatens to damage what remains. Okay, finally the market is going to turn. This frost is going to revive the bull market." But it wasn't to be. The market just slipped right back down again. I never saw the spread trade better than it had on that last Friday in August when I was at Broderick's lake house. The decline was relentless, with only occasional spasms to the upside: up $10,000 one day, down $25,000 the next.

The market continued to grind lower, and I proceeded to lose about $20,000 to $25,000 a day, every day, for months. The clients I advised were sophisticated and experienced traders in their own right, and they had been bailing out of the market since early September. As far as I was concerned, this demonstrated their lack of courage to buy with pride and hold with conviction.

Naturally, I didn't get out. I was in for the long pull. This was going to be the Big Trade. The world was going to run out of bean oil, maybe even mayonnaise, and Smith and I were going to make $10 million.

VERTIGO

For the next several weeks Smith and I kept telling each other, "It's going to be all right. It's gonna turn." Every news story we heard about the market we made fit the "we are going to be okay" scenario. "Now we know why the market was down today. Now that we understand that, it's going to go away. We're going to be okay." We rationalized everything. It was like living in Tortilla Flat with Danny and his friends, rationalizing everything. "Yeah, we just heard that some big commercial firm has just taken some deliveries of bean oil, so if he's stopping them then it must be okay now."

By the beginning of October, I was under water. Soybean prices had fallen to the lowest levels in two months—since the August 11 Agriculture Department crop report predicting a curtailed harvest. Bean oil was now at twenty-nine cents, down from the September highs of thirty-seven cents. I'd lost most of my money. As the position got increasingly worse, I began to get margin calls. I'd be on margin call for two or three days at a time, but the firm's attitude was, "We know you're a big wheel. We know you're on the Executive Committee at the CME, and we know you're neat and you've got this fancy car. We know you're good for the money." I'd wait a few days to see if the market rallied. If it did, fine—I wouldn't have to meet the margin call. If it didn't, I'd spend the next couple of days trying to borrow money from my friends so I could meet the margin call.

I gradually began to lose my outward cool. I was fighting with Pat and the kids; they had no idea what was happening. But it's not uncommon for the spouses and families of traders not to know what's going on with the trader's market positions. I was skipping dinner so I wouldn't have to face my family. I lost fifteen pounds. I couldn't sleep. I was going to bed every night knowing I had to get up the next day and go watch this thing again. It was horrible. It would be a Friday, and I'd say, "Okay, it's Friday. I can't lose any more on this for another couple of days because the market won't be open." Weekends were welcomed. It was exactly opposite of when I was making money on that trade. When I was making money, I couldn't wait for the market to open. When I was losing money, I couldn't wait for it to close. Time is very painful when you're losing money. All I wanted was for the market to rally back to the August highs, and I'd get out.

We refused to accept the obvious: that we were going under. We were holding each other's hands, and every day we went through this little drill of losing an average of $20,000 to $25,000 but telling ourselves that it was going to be all right. Naturally, it never was. It got to be excruciatingly painful. But I couldn't get out of the market because as long as I had the position on, there was always the belief, the chance, the hope, that I could make back the money. If I got out of the market there wouldn't be any chance anymore. "Tomorrow is the first day of the rest of my life. It's going to turn—tomorrow." It was always going to turn "tomorrow." But it never did.

By the first week in November, I was under water big time: $200,000 or $300,000. Bean oil was at twenty-five cents. So from the high of August, I was down about $700,000 or $800,000. What was worse is that I'd borrowed money from my friends to the tune of about $400,000. I got another margin call in mid-November, but I didn't want to borrow any more money from my friends. So I decided to ride out the storm again to see if the market would rally enough to take me off the margin call. On November 17 one of the senior managers from the brokerage firm came into my office and started liquidating my position. The firm finally, and mercifully, pulled the plug on me because I couldn't do it myself.

They not only liquidated the account, but they also started seizing whatever assets I had. They took my membership and sold it, which forced me to resign from the Board of Governors and the Executive Committee since you can't be on the board if you're not a member of the exchange. Then they literally started to take the stuff out of the office: the furniture, the stereo, and the levitating desk and credenza. I can remember sitting at my desk crying as they started to strip the office. It was the absolute lowest point in my life. I had gone from having everything on August 31 to nothing on November 17. I couldn't stand to watch them take all the stuff away, so I took the pictures of my family off the wall, put them in a box, and walked out of the office. I vaguely remember wandering the halls of the exchange for a while trying to figure out what I was going to do. I couldn't borrow any more money from friends, and my only hope for making money had been the bean-oil position. Now it was gone. Well, Pat and I had been through some tough times before; surely we'd make it through this one, too. Oh my God! Pat! How was I going to tell Pat what had happened? How was I going to tell her that my fifteen-year career and all of the money had evaporated in the last two and a half months? I headed for the River Club at the exchange to sort things out over a Jack Daniels.

Several hours, and several drinks, later I weaved my way to the Porsche. I remember deciding the only way I could ever get out of this for my family was to kill myself. I had about a million dollars' worth of life insurance, and the only way I could make it right for my wife and kids was to hit a bridge at 100 m.p.h. I remember thinking to myself, "Everybody knows I drink too much anyway, so it will look like an accident." I thought the insurance company wouldn't pay if it was suicide. I got on the Kennedy Expressway and started looking for a bridge. I had barely even gotten out of the city when I noticed blue lights flashing in my rear-view mirror. I pulled over and waited for the cop to come to the window.

"License and registration, please. Any idea how fast you were going, Mr. Paul?"

"Uh . . . seventy-five? Eighty-five?"

"Try eighteen."

I couldn't believe it. I was so drunk and so dazed over what had happened that I hadn't even gotten out of first gear. I didn't get a speeding ticket. I got a non-speeding ticket, a ticket for careless driving. I was a road hazard because I was doing eighteen m.p.h. on an expressway in a Porsche.

After recovering from the temporary bout of insanity of flirting with suicide, I spent the next three weeks in the house. I refinished the living room floor and did a bunch of other little piddly things around the house. I had to act like I was doing something constructive, so I became Mr. Handyman. That was my "job." I'd have the TV on the financial news channel like I was watching the market and staying abreast of things—even though I didn't have two dimes to put together to do anything about it. I even kept my charts updated, but it was all phony. I wasn't doing anything; I was just acting like I was doing something.

NADIR

After about a month I went to see my old friend from the lumber pit, Stu Gimble. I had no job, no money, and no prospect for either. For some reason Stu wasn't discouraged at all. He thought it was the best thing that could have happened to me. "This is great. We'll get you back on your feet again. All the great traders have gone bust at least once in their careers. You're gonna be fine." He leased and paid the rent on a seat in the Eurodollar pit for me while he tried to teach me to do what he did. A sudden realization was beginning to set in; I wasn't a trader. I couldn't do it. I wasn't good enough. I literally couldn't do what he did, even though I had the best teacher and conceptually understood what he was doing. I wasn't quick enough. He had this fantastic thing for numbers that was unbelievable. But my brain didn't work like his. So there I was in the Eurodollar pit, with no customer business, trying to be a trader and I couldn't make a living.

In September 1984, my accountant figured out that I could refile my previous three years' tax returns, average all three years' income, and get a tax refund. Combining the losses of 1983 with the money I had made in '82 and '81, I got a check from Uncle Sam for about $100,000. That wasn't much money relative to my dire financial situation, but it was a grub stake. The Eurodollar market was so slow and efficient that there just wasn't much price movement. I was used to the lumber market, which really moved a lot, and I thought that whatever I had learned in the lumber pit would apply better to S&Ps than Eurodollars. I bought an IOM (Index and Option Market) seat for $55,000. I was going to try to trade the S&P 500 futures index.

I tried that for five months, and I didn't make any money doing that either. I wasn't any good at it. Once again, this validated that I didn't know how to trade. I tried to rationalize that away, i.e., I hadn't traded in the pit for so long, and I was used to trading from a computer screen in an upstairs office. I sold the seat for $60,000, and that was the last $60,000 I had in the whole world. I hooked back up with Kirby Smith, who was at a small brokerage firm, and we sat in an office every day acting like we were going to trade and make the money back. I played that game until October 1985 and slowly ate up the money. I was still paying for the car, the house, and all the expenses of having a family. You can go through money pretty quickly with those kinds of bills and no money coming in at all.

If I didn't get it together soon, I'd have to get a real job. I'd have to go back to work to survive and keep my family alive. I didn't want to do it since I had come to believe I was above all that. You gotta do what you gotta do. However, I didn't intend to give up on trading. I viewed it like blackjack in the caddy pen; I wasn't going to quit playing, but I was going to quit losing. It was time to be a *smart man*—humbled but resolved to learn from my mistakes.

5

THE QUEST

HOW DO THE PROS MAKE MONEY?

Not only did I lose all of my money because of the stupid way I handled the bean-oil position, but I also discovered that I'd never really been a trader. Sure, I had made money in the markets, but it turned out that I really didn't know how or why I had made it. I couldn't duplicate the profits when I had to make a living strictly by trading. The money I'd made over the years "trading" wasn't because I was a good trader. I'd made money because of being a good salesman, being at the right place at the right time, and knowing the right people, rather than because of some innate trading ability.

It was a painful realization to discover that I wasn't a trader. I didn't have the patience or mechanical skills to be a successful floor trader nor the consistency to be a successful upstairs trader. If I was going to learn how to make money trading I was going to have to find out how others had done it. I went and read the books and articles about and interviews with successful market professionals. I studied the best investors and traders from Wall Street and La Salle Street: Peter Lynch, Bernard Baruch, Jim Rogers, Paul Tudor Jones, Richard Dennis, and many more. After all, when you're sick you want to consult the best doctors, and when you're in trouble you want the advice of the best lawyers. So I consulted what the successful pros had to say about making money in the markets. If I could figure out how they did it, I could still pull off getting rich again. And this time I would keep the money.

Here is some of the advice the pros offered for making money. Appendix A has brief dossier on these pros for those of you not familiar with their names.

ADVICE AND DISSENT

I haven't met a rich technician.[1]
(Jim Rogers)

I always laugh at people who say, 'I've never met a rich technician.' I love that! It is such an arrogant, nonsensical response. I used fundamentals for nine years and then got rich as a technician.[2]
(Marty Schwartz)

Not very encouraging! Okay, so maybe the key to success wasn't whether you were a fundamentalist or a technician. I mean, I had made a lot of money using both of these methods. While I found technical analysis indispensable, there was nothing like a good fundamental situation to really make a market move. Maybe another topic would begin to reveal the pros' secret.

Diversify your investments.[3]
(John Templeton)

All right! Now I was getting somewhere. This was striking a familiar chord. Maybe I had placed too much emphasis on the soybean-oil spreads. I had too large a percentage of my capital committed to that market and that trade. Even afterwards, I was trading only one market at a time. This looked like my first lesson from the masters: diversify. Or it looked that way until I read the following:

Diversification is a hedge for ignorance.[4]
(William O'Neil)

Concentrate your investments. If you have a harem of 40 women you never get to know any of them very well.[5]
(Warren Buffett)

Buffett has made more than $1 billion in the market. Who was I to disagree with him? But Templeton is also one of the greatest investors alive, and he said something totally opposite of Buffett.

Okay, so maybe diversification wasn't the answer either. Maybe you could put all of your eggs in one basket and still get rich by watching the basket very closely. Perhaps the topics I had selected so far were too broad in their implications. Certainly, the pros would agree on the more specific and practical applications of investment and trading mechanics.

AVERAGING A LOSS

You have to understand the business of a company you have invested in, or you will not know whether to buy more if it goes down.[6]
(Peter Lynch)

Averaging down is an amateur strategy that can produce serious losses.[7]
(William O'Neil)

TOP AND BOTTOM PICKING

Don't bottom fish.[8]
(Peter Lynch)

Don't try to buy at the bottom or sell at the top.[9]
(Bernard Baruch)

Maybe the trend is your friend for a few minutes in Chicago, but for the most part it is rarely a way to get rich.[10]

(Jim Rogers)

I believe the very best money is made at the market turns. Everyone says you get killed trying to pick tops and bottoms and you make all the money by catching the trends in the middle. Well, for twelve years I have often been missing the meat in the middle, but I have caught a lot of bottoms and tops.[11]

(Paul Tudor Jones)

SPREADING UP

When you're not sure what is going to happen in the market it is wise to protect yourself by going short in something you think is overvalued.[12]

(Roy Neuberger)

Whether I am bullish or bearish, I always try to have both long and short positions—just in case I'm wrong.[13]

(Jim Rogers)

I have tried being long a stock and short a stock in the same industry but generally found it to be unsuccessful.[14]

(Michael Steinhardt)

Many traders have the idea that when they are in a commodity (or stock), and it starts to decline, they can hedge and protect themselves, that is, short some other commodity (or stock) and make up the loss. There is no greater mistake than this.[15]

(W. D. Gann)

I had expected there might be some subtle differences among the pros. After all, some were stock-market moguls, while others traded options or futures contracts. But didn't these guys agree on anything? Based on the examples above, they sounded more like members of a debate team trying to score points against one another.

I had to find out how the pros made money in the markets. I had to learn the secret that all of them must know. But if the pros couldn't agree on how to make money, how was I going to learn their secret? And then it began to occur to me: there was no secret. They didn't all do the same thing to make money. What one guy said not to do, another guy said you should do. Why didn't they agree? I mean, here was a group of individuals who had collectively taken billions of dollars out of the markets and kept it. Weren't they all doing at least a few things the same when they made their money? Think about it this way; if one guy did what another said not to do, how come the first guy didn't lose his money? And if the first guy hadn't lost, why didn't the second guy?

If imitating the pros was supposed to make you rich and not imitating them was supposed to make you poor, then each one of these guys should have lost all his money because none of them imitated the others. They all should be flat broke because they very often did things opposite of one another. It finally occurred to me that maybe studying losses was more important than searching for some Holy Grail to making money. So I started reading through all the material on the pros again and noted what they had to say about losses.

LOSSES

My basic advice is don't lose money.[16]
(Jim Rogers)

I'm more concerned about controlling the downside. Learn to take the losses. The most important thing in making money is not letting your losses get out of hand.[17]
(Marty Schwartz)

I'm always thinking about losing money as opposed to making money. Don't focus on making money; focus on protecting what you have.[18]
(Paul Tudor Jones)

One investor's two rules of investing:
Never lose money.
Never forget rule #1.[19]
(Warren Buffett)

The majority of unskilled investors stubbornly hold onto their losses when the losses are small and reasonable. They could get out cheaply, but being emotionally involved and human, they keep waiting and hoping until their loss gets much bigger and costs them dearly.[20]
(William O'Neil)

Learn how to take losses quickly and cleanly. Don't expect to be right all the time. If you have a mistake, cut your loss as quickly as possible.[21]
(Bernard Baruch)

Now I was getting somewhere. Why was I trying to learn the secret to making money when it could be done in so many different ways? I knew something about how to make money; I had made a million dollars in the market. But I didn't know anything about how not to lose. The pros could all make money in contradictory ways because they all knew how to control their losses. While one person's method was making money, another person with an opposite approach would be losing—if the second person was in the market. And that's just it; the second person wouldn't be in the market. He'd be on the sidelines with a nominal loss. The pros consider it their primary responsibility not to lose money.

The moral, of course, is that just as there is more than one way to deal blackjack, there is more than one way to make money in the markets. Obviously, there is no secret way to make money because the pros have done it using very different and often contradictory approaches. Learning *how not to lose money* is more important than learning *how to make money.* Unfortunately, the pros didn't explain how to go about acquiring this skill. So I decided to study loss in general, and my losses in particular, to see if I could determine the root causes of losing money in the markets. As I said at the beginning of the book, I may not be wise, but I am now very smart. I eventually did learn from my mistakes.

PART TWO

LESSONS LEARNED

Good judgment is usually the result of experience,
and experience frequently the result of bad judgment.
—ROBERT LOVETT

What started as a search for the secret to making money had turned into a search for the secret of how not to lose money. Why is it is so important to learn how not to lose? Because when people lose money in the markets, they usually look for a new approach to make money. Obviously, the previous method was defective; it's never the investor's or trader's fault. Given the myriad of how-to methods, you could spend a lifetime trying, and failing, to make money with each one because you don't know how not to lose. On the other hand, if you learn why people lose and thereby control losses, profits will follow.

Basically, what I found is that there are as many ways to make money in the markets as there are people in the markets, but there are relatively few ways to lose money. When I say lose here, I don't mean that there won't be any losses. You don't win every point in every game in every set in every match in tennis; you win some and you lose some. There will be lots of losses, just as there are losses in any business. Former Citicorp CEO Walter Wriston said that a lender who doesn't have loan losses isn't doing his job. And it's the truth. Trying to avoid taking losses altogether is the loser's curse. But the losses you are trying to avoid are the ones for which you hadn't made allowances, the ones that sneak up on you and the ones that ultimately put you out of business.

Losing money in the markets is the result of either: (1) some fault in the analysis or (2) some fault in its application. As the pros have demonstrated, there is no single sure-fire analytical way to make money in the markets. Therefore, studying the various analytical methods in search of the "best one" is a waste of time. Instead, what should be studied are the factors involved in applying, or failing to apply, any analytical method. Even when equipped with accurate analysis, correct forecasts, and profitable recommendations, people still manage to lose money. Why can't people match the profitable performance records of the market advisory services they subscribe to? They can't because of psychological factors that prevent them from applying the analysis and following the recommendations.

Psychological factors can be categorized as either (1) the pathological mental disorders and illnesses that require professional help or (2) the psychological distortions all of us engage in even though we are basically mentally healthy. We are interested in the latter.

MARKET LORE TO IGNORE?

Most remedies for market losses due to psychological factors are old market saws that are too ambiguous to offer any means of practical application. People recite these catchphrases as if they were self-evident truths. After repeating them so often they become trite clichés used out of unthinking habit. But pearls of trading wisdom are more easily repeated than implemented. Repeating maxims, as if mere verbalization will activate the underlying principles, will not work. For example, simply following the dictum "Don't discuss market positions because the pros don't," won't automatically make you a pro. You must understand those principles before you can benefit from the maxims. Pros don't discuss their positions *because* they understand what triggers discussing positions in the first place, as well as the dangers of doing so. A maxim is a succinct formulation of some fundamental principle or rule of conduct. Memorizing and repeating clichés is easy; grasping their underlying principles is more difficult.

For instance, consider what must be the most quoted maxim in the business: "Cut your losses short." Sounds great, but what does it mean? Do you get out of a position as soon as it shows a loss? What constitutes a loss? How do you define a market loss? At some point in almost every investment or trade the position is going to show a loss, so how do you know when it is really a *loss*—something to get rid of—and not a position that is going to come back and be profitable?

Or how about: "Don't follow the crowd. Go against the herd." Okay, but how do you measure the crowd's position in the market? What are the truest bellwethers of public sentiment? Do you determine what the crowd is doing by looking at volume and open interest? Put-call ratios? Put-to-call premiums? Consumer confidence? Odd-lot shorts? Sentiment numbers and consensus of investment advisors? Besides, doing the opposite of what everyone else is doing doesn't guarantee success and there are times when "trading opposite the crowd" can wipe you out.

And then there's that oldie but goldie: "Don't trade on hope or fear or make emotional decisions." Sounds simple enough, but as you will see later in the book, emotions in general, and hope and fear specifically, create a unique paradox for the market participant.

This book will not instruct you on the specifics of how to confront your fears or how to "get in touch with your feelings and emotions." It will not reconcile your ego's legitimate internal psychological needs with your participation in the markets. I don't have a battery of tests for you to take to determine your particular psychological profile or your internal conflicts. I don't have a test to determine if you should be participating in the markets at all. I am not, nor do I pretend to be, a psychologist. But I don't have to be a psychologist to know that losses caused by *psychological* factors presuppose your *ego's* involvement in the market position in the first place, which means you have personalized the market. Knowing what causes something is the first step in preventing it from going into effect. If we can determine how a market position gets personalized (i.e., how ego gets involved), we will be well on our way to preventing it from happening. Then the losses due to psychological factors can be prevented.

Some of the ideas in the rest of the book may sound like semantic quibbling. However, it is precisely those confused semantics that are largely responsible for the confused thinking that, in turn, leads to the losses due to psychological factors. To clear up that confusion let's attach clear, specific meanings to the terms we use. Let's start at the beginning by defining psychology and seeing how it applies to us when we are in the market.

The American Heritage Dictionary defines "psychology" as the study of the mental processes, behavioral characteristics, and emotions of an individual or group. Since we're interested in market losses due to psychological factors, we will examine each of the three parts of the definition as they relate to us when we have those types of losses. Therefore, the second part of this book examines the mental processes, behavioral characteristics, and emotions of people who lose money in the markets.

1. Mental Processes

Chapter 6 explains what happens when a market position, especially a loss, gets personalized. It presents the difference between external, objective losses and internal, subjective losses. Next, it looks at the mental process an individual goes through when experiencing an internal loss: denial, anger, bargaining, depression, and acceptance. Most people equate *loss* with *being wrong* and, therefore, internalize what should be an external loss. Then they start to experience the Five Stages of Internal Loss, and the loss gets larger as they progress through the stages. Finally, the chapter makes a distinction between losses from discrete events (e.g., games) and continuous processes (e.g., markets) and shows that only the latter are subject to the Five Stages.

2. Behavioral Characteristics

Chapter 7 discusses the most common way people personalize market positions. The chapter introduces the five types of participants in the markets: investors, traders, speculators, bettors, and gamblers. The type of participant a person is, is determined by the behavioral characteristics he displays, not by the activity in which he is engaged. In other words, all stock purchases are not investing just as all card playing isn't gambling. The chapter also shows that the source of most losses in the markets is people betting or gambling, as defined by the characteristics of their behavior, on a continuous-process risk activity.

3. Emotions of an Individual or Group

Chapter 8 explains that emotions are neither good nor bad; they simply are. Emotions per se cannot be avoided. Emotionalism, on the other hand, can and should be avoided. Emotionalism is decision making based on emotions. The entity that best describes emotional decision making is the crowd. The chapter explains that the crowd is the epitome of emotions in action and discusses the crowd not in the familiar terms of contrary opinion or as a stage of a runaway market but in terms of a process that can affect a solitary individual. Being a member of the crowd is not a function of quantity of people. Rather, it is a function of the characteristics displayed. We will also look at two models that describe the stages an individual passes through as he becomes a member of a psychological crowd.

6

THE PSYCHOLOGICAL
DYNAMICS OF LOSS

I can't get out here; I'm losing too much.

—LOSER'S FAMOUS LAST WORDS

In mid-October 1983, while the bean-oil position was blowing up in my face, I got a call from my mom. "Dad is going into the hospital for exploratory cancer surgery. It shouldn't be a big deal and they don't expect a problem, but they have to take a look," she said. She called back the next day after the surgery, and the news from the doctors was that the cancer had spread through his whole body and he had six months to live. They'd given him a full colostomy and he would start going to start chemo-radiation therapy immediately.

Two months later I got a call from my dad. He said, "Mom's gone. I can't find her. She left last night and hasn't come home." As it turned out, my mom had committed suicide. She had walked into the Ohio River and drowned herself. The only good news was that she didn't know I was broke, so it wasn't my situation that made her do it. She did it because my dad was so sick and going to die and she couldn't deal with it. I'd really have been in bad shape if I'd thought that she did it because of my situation. But they had no idea that I'd gone under. Things didn't look any different. We still lived in the house and so on. I just didn't have the same job. They knew I'd had a job change, but they didn't know why.

By that time my dad was in and out of the nursing home and had a full-time nurse at home. I was driving back and forth almost every weekend *visiting him and watching him die. I would go one weekend, and my brother would go the next. Finally, in August of 1984 he died.*

So between August 1983 and August 1984, I lost all of my money; went $400,000 in debt; lost my membership, my job, my Board of Governor's seat, my Executive Committee seat, and both of my parents. I lost everything that was important to me except my wife and kids. That was not a good twelve months.

I am not relating this story for your pity. I am relating it because it helps convey some important observations I made about the nature of loss. My losses in the market weren't the same as the losses in my personal life. My gambling losses in Las Vegas weren't the same as losses in the markets. All those losses were different from the loss of my parents, which was different from losing my Board of Governors seat.

Most people acknowledge that losses will happen regardless of the type of business venture. A light-bulb manufacturer knows that two out of three hundred bulbs will break. A fruit dealer knows that two out of one hundred apples will rot. Losses per se don't bother them; unexpected losses and losing on balance does. Acknowledging that losses are part of business is one thing; taking and accepting those losses in the markets is something else entirely. In the markets, people tend to have difficulty actively (as opposed to passively, as in the case of the fruit dealer and bulb manufacturer) taking losses (i.e., accepting and controlling losses so that the business venture itself doesn't become a loser). This is because all losses are treated as failure; in every other area of our lives, the word *loss* has negative connotations. People tend to regard the words *loss*, *wrong*, *bad*, and *failure* as the same, and *win*, *right*, *good*, and *success* as the same. For instance, we *lose* points for *wrong* answers on tests in school. Likewise, when we lose money in the market we think we must have been wrong.

The American Heritage Dictionary defines *lose* as (1) to be deprived of through death and (2) to fail to win (i.e., to lose a game; to be defeated). Most of the time *lose* or *loss* is associated with games. Somehow, the concepts *profit* and *loss* get confused with *win* and *lose* and *right* and *wrong*. But if you *lose* as a participant of a game, you weren't wrong; you were defeated. If you lose as a spectator of a game, you must have placed a bet (or expressed an opinion) on the game's outcome and you lost money (or were wrong), but you were not defeated.

EXTERNAL VS. INTERNAL LOSSES

There are many different types of losses. You can lose your keys, a game or contest, money, your mind, esteem, self-control, your parents, a bet, a job, etc. However, all losses can be categorized either as (1) internal, such as self-control, esteem, love, your mind, or (2) external, such as a bet, a game or contest, money. External losses are objective, and internal losses are subjective. That is, an external loss is not open to subjective, individual interpretation; it is an objective fact. On the other hand, an internal loss is defined in terms of the individual (i.e., subject) experiencing it. In other words, a loss is objective when it is the same for me, you, and anyone else. The loss is subjective when it differs from one person to another, when it is entirely a personal experience.

For instance, thousands of people die every day, but those deaths aren't "losses" to everyone, only to those who are directly and personally (i.e., internally and emotionally) affected. This type of loss is an internal loss and is a function of, and created by, the feelings and reactions of the person experiencing them. This means the loss is *subjective* and definable only in terms of the individual experiencing it. On the other hand, when Kentucky loses a basketball game, it is no more of a loss for a member of the losing team than for a spectator in terms of it being an external, *objective* fact. Both people are totally outside the definition of the event itself. Anyone who was watching the game can tell you which team lost, and everyone watching would tell you the same thing. An objective loss is impervious to how you feel about it or react to it. It's not subject to anyone's appraisal; it must be accepted without evaluation. The player and spectator just mentioned *could* personalize this external loss *if* they equated their self-esteem with the success or failure of the team. This would internalize an external loss.

Because people tend to regard *loss*, *wrong*, *bad*, and *failure* as the same thing, it is little wonder that *loss* is a dirty word in our vocabulary. However, in the markets losses should be viewed like the light bulbs or rotten fruit mentioned earlier: part of the business and taken with equanimity. *Loss* is not the same as *wrong*, and *loss* is not necessarily *bad*. For example, consider exiting a losing position with a small loss but before the loss got bigger. That was a loss, but it was a good decision. By the same token, a profitable trade based on a tip may be bad because of the dangers of following tips (i.e., the tipster may have incorrect information or he doesn't tell you when to get out).

Market losses are external, objective losses. It's only when you internalize the loss that it becomes subjective. This involves your ego and causes you to view it in a negative way, as a failure, something that is wrong or bad. Since psychology deals with your ego, if you can eliminate ego from the decision-making process, you can begin to control the losses caused by psychological factors. The trick to preventing market losses from becoming internal losses is to understand how it happens and then avoid those processes.

HOW MARKET LOSSES BECOME INTERNAL LOSSES

The key to understanding how external losses become internalized lies in knowing the subtle differences between facts and opinions. *The American Heritage Dictionary* defines a *fact* as something that has been objectively verified. Facts are neither right nor wrong; they simply are. Opinions are personal assessments and are right or wrong depending on whether they actually correspond with the facts. Therefore, only opinions can be right or wrong; facts cannot. *Right* and *wrong* are inappropriate for the description of business operations and market participation, and so are the terms *win* and *lose*. Participating in markets is not about being right or wrong, nor is it about defeat; it's about making decisions.

Decision making is a process of reaching a conclusion after careful consideration; it is a judgment, a choice between alternatives when all the facts are not yet, and cannot yet, be known because they depend on events unfolding in the future. Therefore, decision making is not a choice between right and wrong. In 20/20 hindsight, decisions might be *good* or *bad* but not *right* or *wrong*. With regard to the markets, only expressed opinions can be right or wrong. Market positions are either *profitable* or *unprofitable*, period. But due to the vocabulary quirks outlined above, it is easy to equate *losing* money in the market with being *wrong*. In doing so, you take what had been a decision about money (external) and make it a matter of reputation and pride (internal). This is how your ego gets involved in the position. You begin to take the market personally, which takes the loss from being objective to being subjective. It is no longer a loss of money, but a personal loss to you (i.e., someone you knew was on the airplane that crashed). An example of personalizing market positions is people's tendency to exit profitable positions and keep unprofitable positions. It's as if profits and losses were a reflection of their intelligence or self-worth; if they *take* the loss it will make them feel stupid or wrong. They confuse net worth with self-worth.

The very use of the terms *right* and *wrong* when describing a market position or business dealing means (1) an opinion has been expressed, which only a person can do; (2) the market position or business venture has been personalized; and (3) any losses (or successes) are going to be internalized. Remember when I described the high from *being right* about the market on my $248,000 day? "I" had just made all that money for me and everyone else. "I" was so smart. I didn't know it at the time, but the only thing "I" had done was completely personalize my position in the market.

THE FIVE STAGES OF INTERNAL LOSS

It may seem a bit strange comparing the loss of life to a loss in the market. Ordinarily, you wouldn't think of a loss in the market as a life-or-death situation (although living through a million-and-a-half-dollar loss can sure make you think about the alternative). However, the stages people go through when experiencing a loss in the market are strikingly similar to the stages people go through when facing death. When my father was dying, a friend of mine gave me a book about people with terminal illnesses titled *On Death and Dying*, by Elisabeth Kübler-Ross. During interviews with 200 terminally ill patients, the author identified five stages terminally ill patients go through once they find out about their illness. One can see the same stages in most people facing personally tragic news, such as the death of a spouse or a child. I also think people experiencing any type of internal loss go through these stages. For the purposes of this book let's refer to them as the Five Stages of Internal Loss. Below is a brief description of each stage and a reference to how I displayed the same characteristics when I was in the bean-oil trade.

1. Denial

Upon receiving the news of being terminally ill, patients immediately responded, "No, not me. It can't be true." Some patients were observed "shopping around" for many doctors, looking for reassuring second opinions. Patients discounted doctors' opinions that confirmed the original diagnosis and emphasized those that were more optimistic.

This is the same thing I was doing in September and October of 1983 when the bean-oil position stopped going up and started down. I was losing money but denied that the market had really turned around. I was indignant. That was the trade that was going to make me $10 million, remember? In October I knew that I was under water but didn't even know how far under I was. That is the personification of denial. If you can't even, or don't dare, sit down and calculate how much you're losing in a position, but you know to the exact penny how much you're making on your profitable positions, then you're denying the loss. I also sought "second opinions" by asking other traders what they thought about the market. And, of course, I listened to the ones who were bullish and ignored those who weren't.

2. Anger

When the denial stage cannot be maintained any longer, it is replaced with feelings of anger (e.g., rage, envy, resentment). The anger is displaced in all directions (e.g., nurse, family, doctor, treatment) and projected onto the environment at random. I vented a lot of my frustrations about the loss in the form of anger directed mainly at my family. For a while, Pat and the kids avoided me like the plague.

3. Bargaining

Unable to face facts in the first stage and angry at people and God in the second stage, patients try to succeed in entering some sort of agreement that may postpone the inevitable from happening: "If God has decided to take me from this earth, and he did not respond to my angry pleas, he may be more favorable if I ask nicely." In September 1983 I made a pact with myself that if the market rallied back to where it had been in late August I'd get out of the position. By November I was begging the market just to get my position back to breakeven. All I wanted to do was get back to where I was before I had put on the bean-oil trade.

4. Depression

Depression is a complex psychological disorder, and discussing it at length is beyond the scope of this book. Generally speaking, however, some of the symptoms of depression are pervasive feelings of sadness, distancing yourself from loved ones, changes in appetite or sleep habits, loss of energy, inability to concentrate, indecisiveness, and refusal to follow advice. While I never went to a doctor to see if I was clinically depressed, I had a lot of these symptoms in the fall of 1983. I was so consumed with the bean-oil position that I couldn't sleep through the night, skipped meals, lost fifteen pounds in four weeks, and lost interest in all the things that I once had found enjoyable. I was constantly tired, couldn't focus on my work, and refused the advice of those who told me to get out of the market.

5. Acceptance

The patient finally resigns himself to the inevitable. In this stage, communication becomes more nonverbal. Kübler-Ross says acceptance is almost void of any feelings and is marked by resignation. There are patients who fight to the end, who struggle and keep a hope that makes it almost impossible to reach the stage of acceptance. The harder the struggle to avoid the inevitable death and the more they try to deny it, the more difficult it will be for them to reach this final stage. But they do finally reach this stage. Similarly, the trader finally faces up to the inescapable reality and "accepts" the loss, either because he "wakes up" and does something to get out of the position or, more likely, because someone or something else forces him to exit the position. In my case, it was the latter. Without force I never would have accepted, nor taken, the loss.

For terminally ill patients, the one thing that usually persists through all these stages is hope. Even the most accepting patients left open the possibility for some cure, the discovery of a new drug or last-minute success in a research project. They showed the greatest confidence in the doctors who allowed for such hope and appreciated it when hope was offered in spite of bad news. This is the same hope I was relying on when the bean-oil position was deteriorating. When I talked to other traders, I only paid attention to the opinions and the news that confirmed my position in the market.

THE FIVE STAGES OF INTERNAL LOSS
AND THE MARKET PARTICIPANT

Once a person has personalized a market position and it starts to show a loss, he is uncertain when or how it is going to end (just like the person with the terminal illness is uncertain what's coming next) and he goes through the Five Stages of Internal Loss. He denies it's a loss. ("No way! Is the market really down there? Are you sure that's not a misprint?") It's a profitable trade that just hasn't gone his way yet. He gets angry at his broker or his spouse or the market. After that he starts bargaining with God or the market—that if he can only get back to breakeven, he will get out of the position. Then he gets depressed about the losing position. Finally, acceptance comes either because he "wakes up," the analyst finally puts out a sell recommendation, or the margin clerk blows him out of the position.

The market participant doesn't have to move directly to the acceptance stage. He can loop back to denial after each and every temporary reprieve the market gives him. If the market rallies some, he thinks the market has finally turned. But when the market starts back down again, he slips back into denial, then anger, and so on. With each temporary rally he has another opportunity to play out the stages and lose more money in the process.

Even if the position is a net profit, the trader or investor can go through the Five Stages. Consider when a market position is profitable but not as profitable as it once was. When that happens, he becomes married to the price at which it was the most profitable. He denies that the move is over, gets angry when the market starts to sell off, makes a bargain that he'll get out if the market moves back to that arbitrary point, gets depressed that he didn't get out, and maybe even lets the profit turn into a loss, thus slipping again into denial, then anger, etc. He creates a chain reaction of loops that result in further losses.

This is exactly what I did in the bean-oil trade. Every time the market rallied, I felt relieved and assumed that the decline was over. Having survived each downdraft, I would start looking at the market as though I had just entered the position, and I would create new levels and parameters with which to monitor the market.

DISCRETE EVENTS VS. CONTINUOUS PROCESSES

Earlier in the chapter we saw that someone could actually internalize an external loss; the player or spectator *could* take the loss of the game as a personal matter and internalize what is properly an external loss. Although someone *could* do it, it's a little hard to imagine someone going through the stages of denial, anger, bargaining, depression, and acceptance over a basketball game. Why? Because the game is a *discrete event*—an activity with a defined ending point. However, internalizing an external loss is a lot easier to do with the other type of loss-producing activity: a *continuous process*—an activity that has no clearly defined end. Losses from continuous processes are much more prone to become internalized because, like all internal losses, there is no predetermined ending point.

In a continuous process, the participant gets to continuously make and remake decisions that can affect how much money he makes or loses. On the other hand, a discrete event (e.g., a football game, roulette, blackjack, or other casino game) has a defined ending point, which is characteristic of external losses. A loss resulting from a discrete event is definitive and not open to interpretation. When I bet on a Kentucky basketball game and Kentucky loses, it is a discrete event and an external loss that I can't really argue with. Or, if I bet on 21 red in roulette and the ball lands on 17 black, I lost—period.

The markets fall into the category of continuous process because market positions have no predetermined ending point. Granted, the market has a defined open and close for the day, but a market position continues beyond the market's close and could go on forever. Even though a loss in the market is an external loss (since money is external, not internal), it is also the result of a continuous process and prone to becoming an internal loss. Why? In a continuous process there is no certainty of how or when the open market position will end. That uncertainty about the future triggers the Five Stages of Internal Loss, which means the loss has become internalized, personalized, and subjective. Because a losing market position is a continuous process, nothing forces you to acknowledge it as a loss; there's just you, your money, and the market as a silent thief. So as long as your money holds out, you can continue to kid yourself that the position is a winner that just hasn't gone your way yet. The position may be losing money, but you tell yourself it's not a loss because you haven't closed the position yet. This is especially true for stock-market positions because when you own the stock outright, no margin call is going to force you to call a loss a loss.

Think of the differences between discrete events and continuous processes this way: Would you lose more money or less money at the racetrack if they stopped the race in the middle and reopened the betting window? That is to say, if you had the opportunity to either (1) leave your bet or (2) make a second bet on another horse. You sat down before the race looked at the racing form and said, "Okay, number 4 is obviously the class horse, but he's three to two and I'm not going to bet the favorite because there's not enough payoff. I kind of like number 7, and he's five to three, but 9 looks okay and he's seven to one. I'll go with 9." Half way through the race who's in front? Number 7. If they could stop the race and let you bet again, what would you do? You would say, "I knew it! I liked 7 to begin with. I should have picked 7." You would go to the betting window and make a new bet on number 7. Who wins? Number 4. In the markets they never close the window. It's open all the time, so you continuously get to remake that decision and constantly make new "bets."

When I was in Cleveland managing the office for Jack Salmon's regional firm, I had an experience that demonstrates this concept of internalizing external losses. One time a lot of my customers got short the lumber market. They were big cash lumber hedgers and knew that market as well as anybody. Their analysis, and mine too, was that the market was overpriced and due for a fall. So we got short. Well, the market rallied sharply. The market opened limit up and stayed limit up for four days in a row. There was no trading in the futures so we couldn't get out of our shorts. On the fifth day, the market started to trade but we didn't get out. We wanted to watch the market to see if it would start back down. Well, it didn't. After a few more days of the market trading during the day but closing limit up, we all got out of our shorts. God, it was awful. It had wiped out 90 percent of the office equity run.

I called Jack Salmon down in St. Louis. "Look, I just blew up the office. There is no more money; no more business. It's all gone. I've destroyed it."

"What happened?"

"We were short lumber, and the market kept going up and—"

"Well, whose idea was the trade?"

"It was the customers' idea, but—"

"Okay, how many lawsuits do we have?"

"We don't have any lawsuits. These guys are good guys; they're not going to sue anybody. But—"

"How many debits do we have?"

"We don't have any debits! Don't you understand? We lost all the money!"

"Wait a minute. Let me see if I understand this. We have no lawsuits, no debits, and no customer complaints."

"Right."

"Well, that just means you've got to go back to work, boy. You've got to pick up the phone again. This is part of the business. This is part of the deal. People get on the wrong side of the market and they lose all their money. Then the broker has to decide, 'Do I want to stay in the business of get out of the business?' Want to get out? Get out. Want to stay in? You don't have any problems—you just have to go back to work."

Not only had I failed to see that losses were just part of business, but I had gone so far as to personalize someone else's losses. If only I had known then what I'm writing now . . .

7

THE PSYCHOLOGICAL
FALLACIES OF RISK

Most people who think they are investing are speculating.
And most people who think they are speculating are gambling.

—UNKNOWN

One day in the summer of 1981, my partner Larry Broderick and I met in Las Vegas with one of our best customers—Conrad Pinette, a French Canadian and the manager of a very large lumber company in Canada. He was very wealthy and a big baccarat player. We got to Vegas and checked into the Hilton, since that's where Conrad liked to stay. This was the first trip to the Las Vegas Hilton for Larry and me, and they didn't know us from Adam's off ox; but they knew Conrad. He was a very big player and they loved him. All they want in Vegas is a guy who will play, and Conrad would play.

We met Conrad in the hotel lobby and the first thing he said was, "What kind of a line do you boys want?" I said, "I don't know." "Well, why don't I just get you set up for ten thousand?" "Ten thousand? Dollars?" I really didn't want to lose $10,000. "Ah, we'll just set you up with a line. Don't worry about it." So when I got to the casino all I had to do was sign a piece of paper and they gave me two or three thousand dollars in chips. I just signed and they gave me chips. "Hey, this is kind of neat," I thought to myself. It's not like I even had to have the money.

Conrad wanted to "warm up" before going to play baccarat. His warm-up was to sit down at a blackjack table with a fifty-dollar minimum bet. Now this was at a time when I might have been trading twenty or thirty or *forty contracts at a crack as a local trader. On twenty contracts I might be making or losing $1,000, $3,000, or even $5,000 in an hour in the pit.*

Serious money. So in context, fifty-dollar blackjack wasn't a lot of money. But when I sat down at that table, fifty dollars sure seemed like an awful lot of money. I said to myself, "What am I doing betting fifty dollars? This is nuts." But he was the customer, and Larry and I wanted to make him happy. Well, in half an hour I was down about $500 playing warm-up. I said, "Eh, this is not good . . . I'm not having fun here. I've had it with this warm-up stuff. Let's go try this baccarat thing."

Baccarat was neat. It's been a game for the rich in France and Italy since the fifteenth century. I was rich in 1981, so I wanted to play. In the casinos it's always off to the side. It's roped off, and they have to unfasten a velvet rope to let you in. It's where the big guys play. The riffraff was out there throwing craps and playing roulette, and the big boys were in here at the fancy table where the waitresses catered to you and got you anything you wanted to drink. They served you brand-name drinks at the baccarat table. I liked that.

A guy met us at the velvet rope and said, "Mr. Pinette, Mr. Paul, Mr. Broderick, we're glad to have you." We sat down and signed a little piece of paper, and the guy shoved a whole bunch of chips in front of us. I had never played baccarat before, but I'd read about it in the James Bond book Goldfinger. *The first thing you learn about baccarat is that there really are no decisions to make other than which way to bet (Player, House, or Tie) and how much to bet. In blackjack, you're making choices—do you want a card or not?—in addition to how much you want to bet. In baccarat there are no decisions about the cards; the rules make all the decisions. The game is determined entirely by chance. The dealer deals two cards to the two sides (House and Player) and the rules dictate whether or not a third card is drawn. The object of the game is to draw cards adding to nine (tens and face cards count as zero). The dealer makes sure the bettors follow the inflexible rules.*

The strategy of baccarat players is similar to what traders use in the markets; they look for trends. The players get a little scorecard. Across the top it says House, Player, and Tie, and it has columns under the headings. After every hand they put a little "x" under the appropriate heading, depending on who won. What they're looking for is a run of wins by either the House or Player. So if the House wins three straight hands, for instance, they will bet on the House on the fourth hand. Conrad was explaining all this stuff, most of which made little sense to me. But he was the hot-shot gambler and supposedly knew what he was doing.

So I started playing the "look for the run" routine and betting the minimum twenty-five dollars. Well, somewhere along the line I was down about $2,000 with this Mickey Mouse looking for runs. I was getting very bored and more than a little upset. Two thousand dollars is real money. I don't know what else I would have done with two grand but I can think of a lot of things I could have done, like bought two pairs of Lucchese boots or a new shotgun.

Well, at about three o'clock in the morning we got a new dealer and a new dealing shoe. The first two hands in the new shoe came up Player. Conrad looked at us and said, "Guys. This is it. I feel it. This is it. We're gonna get a run." So he doubled his bet (he was betting $100 or $200 at a crack). I still bet my twenty-five dollars and we bet on Player. Player won the third hand. I left the fifty dollars. Player won again. I left the hundred dollars. Player won again! Well, before the run ended Player had won sixteen straight hands. Luckily for us, somewhere around the tenth or eleventh hand we started taking some money off of the table and lowering our bets. Conrad made about $40,000. Broderick and I each made about $7,000.

Now, it was four o'clock in the morning in Las Vegas, and we had all this free money that had just shown up out of the sky! You can get into a lot of trouble in Las Vegas with that much free money that you don't need, didn't expect to have, and don't care if you have the next day.

Life is fraught with risk. Crossing the street is a risk, driving a car is a risk, getting married is a risk, and so is having children. Needless to say, starting and operating a business is a risk, and so is participating in the markets. Risk is defined as the *possibility* of suffering a loss. (It's called *probability* only if you can assign a numerical value to the likelihood of the loss occurring.) In none of life's activities is there a guarantee of success or of having things turn out the way you want. Obviously, the types of risk we are interested in are financial in nature, risk that produces monetary losses.

Most people don't know whether they are investing, speculating, or gambling, and to the untrained eye the activities are very similar. Looking back on my trip to Vegas I can see the similarity between the casino and the brokerage house. The brokers are the croupiers. The commissions are similar to the house percentage. The boardrooms are the casinos themselves. The stock exchange and the ticker tape are the gambling devices.[1] However, the markets and gambling games are similar only in that they each involve the possibility of monetary loss. They are different not only in the legal sense but also in the economic sense. The big difference is: gambling creates risk while investing/speculating assumes and manages risk that already exists.

INHERENT RISK

Inherent risk is a natural occurrence in both unorganized markets and organized markets. Management guru Peter Drucker calls it "risk which is coincident with the commitment of present resources to future expectations."[2] Unorganized markets are the everyday markets in which we participate as consumers, such as the department store, the grocery store, and the gas station. The producers bear the financial risks associated with getting the product to the consumer. Organized markets, on the other hand, are the centralized exchanges and over-the-counter markets for stocks, bonds, currencies, options, and futures contracts.

CREATED RISK

Created risk involves the arbitrary invention of a potential monetary loss that otherwise would not have existed. Created risk is risk that is not a natural by-product of an activity itself. The roulette wheel could be spun, the football game played, and the horse race run without monetary loss occurring.

Generally speaking, that's as far as people distinguish between inherent and created risk. However, a closer examination reveals that what determines whether someone is engaging in created or inherent risk is not the activity itself but the characteristics the person exhibits when engaging in the activity.

Let's define what those five activities are and the characteristics associated with each.

1. Investing is parting with capital in the expectation of safety of principal and an adequate return on the capital in the form of dividends, interest, or rent. Since the return on capital takes the form of periodic payments of interest or dividends, investing indicates an intention to be separated from the capital for an extended period of time. Therefore, investing is usually associated with relatively long time horizon. Buying stocks in a pension fund with the intention of holding them indefinitely or buying bonds with the intention of holding until maturity is investing.

2. Trading is basically an activity in which someone (usually called a dealer) makes a market in a given financial instrument. Traders try to extract the bid-ask spread from a market. An example of a trader is the specialist on the floor of a stock exchange. He matches orders, maintains an orderly market and is willing to buy at the bid and sell at the offer. Traders on the futures and options exchanges make two-sided markets, trying to buy at the bid and sell at the offer. Traders in the over-the-counter stock and bond markets do the same thing. In its most basic definition, trading is market making. The trader essentially tries to stay net flat (neither long nor short) and makes money by extracting the bid-ask spread. In this sense, Stu Gimble, my friend from the lumber and Eurodollar pits, was the consummate mechanical trader.

3. Speculating in its simplest form is buying for resale rather than for use or income as is the case for commodities or financial instruments, respectively. Speculating is parting with capital in the expectation of capital appreciation. This capital appreciation is the sole extent of "return" for the speculator. He does not anticipate

return in the form of periodic dividends or interest payments because he does not intend to hold the position for an extended period of time. The word speculation is derived from the Latin word *specere*, which means "to see." Speculating means vision, perception, the faculty of intellectual examination.

4. Betting is an agreement between two parties where the party proved *wrong* about the outcome of an uncertain event will forfeit a stipulated thing or sum to the other party. Therefore, a bet is about being *right* or *wrong*. For example, people bet on the result of an election or a football game. More often than not, they bet on whom they want to win rather than on whom they think will win. I always bet on Kentucky in basketball games. If I took into account the point spread, that would be speculating. If I had been a bookie taking bets either way, trying to keep my exposure even and extracting my commission, I would have been more like a trader who tries to stay net flat and extracts the bid-ask spread.

5. Gambling is a derivative of betting. To gamble is to wager money on the outcome of a game, contest, or event or to play a game of chance for money or other stakes. Gambling usually involves a game or event of chance; sometimes it involves games of both skill and chance. While gambling is popularly regarded as a vice that is injurious to public morals, it is actually a form of entertainment. Compulsive gambling might be injurious, but so is compulsive behavior of any kind. Gamblers may make money, but they are not deprived of enjoyment or entertainment if they do not make money. Individuals who lose a couple of hundred dollars in casinos are paying an entertainment fee, and they know it and have decided it's worth it. They engage in the activity for the action and the excitement of participation.

BEHAVIORAL CHARACTERISTICS DETERMINE THE ACTIVITY

Don't make the mistake of assuming that just because you're participating in the market you are automatically investing, trading, or speculating. The markets don't make you immune from betting or gambling. Determining which of the five activities you are doing is a function of the behavioral characteristics you exhibit. Gambling, investing, and trading are not defined by any particular activity itself (i.e., playing cards, buying stocks, or trading futures) but by how the person approaches the activity. All card playing is not gambling, all stock purchases are not investing, and all futures transactions are not trading.

Gambling and betting are most often associated with contests or games, such as casino games, sports games, horse racing, slot machines, and bingo, to name a few. Bettors and gamblers can be either spectators or participants in the event on which they wager. But the distinguishing characteristic of a bettor or a gambler is whether he wants the satisfaction of being right in his prediction or the *entertainment* of participating, respectively.

The bettor is interested in being right. His ego is on the line. He has a stalwart fealty to a team, a market position, or an opinion. Very often, market analysts are subject to this pitfall. Having expressed an opinion either on market direction or the value of a particular stock, it becomes difficult, if not impossible, to abandon that opinion. The analyst doesn't want to be wrong or look stupid; he wants to be right. He is betting.

The immediate aim of gambling is entertainment, betting for excitement. People gamble to escape the humdrum of everyday life. It fulfills the desire for stimulus (e.g., increased adrenaline and a rise in blood pressure) replacing the painful boredom of everyday life with thrill or excitement. The distinguishing feature of gambling is that it deals with the unknown, with pure chance. Money is only the ticket to this game, and, therefore, winning or losing is relatively unimportant. It's the excitement that's important in gambling, the way right and wrong are important in betting, the way money is important in investing, trading, and speculating. In gambling, winning is desired only in that money is needed to enter the game or continue playing; money is good for only one thing and that is to gamble.

Conventional gambling serves no purposes other than those common to other forms of play. The gambler isn't playing a game; he is just playing. To a gambler, all normal criteria of odds (respective return, probability of winning, etc.) are irrelevant. At the poker table you always see some guy who stays in every hand, going for the inside straight even though the odds are he's not going to hit it. In a best case situation, the odds are twelve to one against him and deteriorate from there if one of the cards he needs has already been played or is in another player's hand. When I was in Las Vegas with Larry and Conrad, I saw gamblers at the roulette table just throwing money away. But they didn't care; they were interested in entertainment and excitement, not money.

It is important to understand that not all participants in gambling games are gamblers. The aim of the "professional gambler," as he is called, is to make money. He can be recognized by deliberate and extremely disciplined wagering. His wagering is systematic and usually limited to infrequent but highly favorable opportunities. The behavior of the professional gambler is highly controlled and usually the result of a studied approach to his chosen game. He concentrates on games where the element of skill is sufficient to produce the possibility of a player advantage, such as blackjack and parimutuel betting. The professional gambler is similar to the stock arbitrageur in that they both take calculated risks. They are dealing with an uncertain outcome and seek to profit from their ability to anticipate the future or to *see the future*—in other words, to speculate. Professional gamblers are actually speculators because of the characteristics they exhibit when risking money. They are not seeking entertainment at the tables like gamblers do, and they are not trying to be right. They are trying to make money.

Consider Edward O. Thorp, the author of *Beat the Dealer* and a mathematics professor who devised a winning card-counting system on a high-speed computer. He won so much money in Las Vegas playing blackjack that the Vegas Resort Hotel Association changed the rules of the game. Thorp wasn't gambling, even though he was playing cards. He was a professional speculator. Or consider a story reported in *Business Week* about an entrepreneur who started a small service company, took it public, made $20 million, and then turned around and lost it in another business venture. He said "the relationship between gambling and entrepreneurship was an uneasy one" and confessed to behaving like a gambler in a business enterprise.[3] This guy wasn't speculating on a business venture—he was gambling and fell prey to "gambler's ruin." That is, he wagered it all on that one venture just as I had wagered disproportionately on the bean-oil trade. If a person approaches a business risk or a risk in the financial markets for excitement, then he is gambling—regardless of how much control he supposedly has over the outcome.

If you can find speculators in casinos, then you can also find gamblers and bettors in the stock and commodity markets either as customers, brokers, or analysts. Whether they are betting or gambling is a function of how they go about participating in the markets. Are they exhibiting the characteristics of a bettor or gambler? If so, then they are betting or gambling—regardless of what they think they are doing or say they are doing.

A DANGEROUS COMBINATION

As the epigraph to this chapter indicates, most people don't know whether they are engaging in inherent- or created-risk activities. Couple this with people's failure to distinguish between the two types of loss-producing events, continuous and discrete, introduced at the end of the last chapter, and you have a disaster waiting to happen. Recall that in discrete events, such as gambling and betting games, there is a defined end to the risk activity. But inherent-risk activities are continuous processes with no predetermined end. For instance, running a business keeps you continuously exposed to the risks coincident with the commitment of resources to future expectations. A single sales transaction may be a defined event with a beginning and an end, but the business operation itself is a continuous process. Likewise, a market position is a continuous process, which introduces the possibility of internal losses because of the uncertainty of when the process will end. On the other hand, created-risk activities are associated with discrete events, such as sports games, political contests, or the rolls of the dice; the game ends, the contest finishes, and the dice stop rolling.

Betting and gambling are suitable for discrete events but not for continuous processes. If you introduce the behavioral characteristics of betting or gambling into a continuous process, you are leaving yourself open to enormous losses. In betting and gambling games, you wager and wait to see if you are right or to experience some excitement, respectively. Any resulting monetary losses are real, but they are also passive because the discrete event ends all by itself. On the other hand, a position in the market is a continuous process that doesn't end until you make it end. If you "wager and wait" in the market, you can lose a lot of money. In betting and gambling games if you stop acting and do nothing, the losses will stop. But when investing, trading, or speculating, if you're losing and stop acting, the losses don't stop; they can continue to grow almost indefinitely.

PSYCHOLOGICAL FALLACIES

We've already seen that everyday life involves risk. Likewise, estimating and managing those risks is a necessary part of everyday life. Probability is the mathematics of estimating risk, and you know how I feel about math. I'm not going into a long dissertation on the subject. I am, however, going to point out some of the more common misunderstandings about probability and how we psychologically distort situations to make the odds seem more in our favor. In this section, I want to point out a few examples of the fallacies in popularly held beliefs about probability and how market participants apply the same fallacies to their market strategies and positions. Succumbing to the fallacies is harmful enough when applied to discrete events, but it is catastrophic when applied to continuous processes. Below are a few examples of the psychological fallacies most people have when it comes to risk and probability.[4]

1. The first psychological fallacy is the tendency to overvalue wagers involving a low probability of a high gain and to undervalue wagers involving a relatively high probability of low gain. The best examples are the favorites and the long shots at racetracks.

2. The second is a tendency to interpret the probability of successive independent events as additive rather than multiplicative. In other words, people view the chance of throwing a given number on a die to be twice as large with two throws as it is with a single throw—like throwing sixes four times in a row in craps and thinking that must mean their chances of throwing a seven next have improved.

3. The third is the belief that after a run of successes, a failure is mathematically inevitable, and vice versa. This is known as the Monte Carlo fallacy. A person can throw double sixes in craps ten times in a row and not violate any laws of probability because each of the throws is independent of all others.

4. Fourth is the perception that the psychological probability of the occurrence of an event exceeds the mathematical probability if the event is favorable and vice versa. For example, the probability of success of drawing the winning ticket in the lottery and the probability of being killed by lightning may both be one in 10,000, yet from a personal viewpoint, buying the winning lottery ticket is considered much more probable than getting hit by lightning.

5. Fifth is people's tendency to overestimate the frequency of the occurrence of infrequent events and to underestimate that of comparatively frequent ones after observing a series of randomly generated events of different kinds with an interest in the frequency with which each kind of event occurs. Thus, they remember the "streaks" in a long series of wins and losses and tend to minimize the number of short-term runs.

6. Sixth is people's tendency to confuse the occurrence of "unusual" events with the occurrence of low-probability events. For example, the remarkable feature of a bridge hand of thirteen spades is its apparent regularity, not its rarity (all hands are equally probable). As another example, if one holds a number close to the winning num-

ber in a lottery, he tends to feel that a terrible bad stroke of misfortune has caused him just to miss the prize.

SOME EXAMPLES

Independent Events

A dealing shoe in baccarat doesn't know anything about what cards have already been dealt. Cards coming out of a deck are statistically independent events. In fact, one might argue that according to the law of large numbers, each side has a fifty-fifty probability of winning and one should bet against the run in baccarat. Nevertheless, people bet in baccarat on the premise that the random events of drawing cards from a dealing shoe are somehow related to one another and will tend to create a string of runs.

Risk, Exposure, and Probability

The definition of risk is to expose to the *chance* or *possibility* of loss. Most people erroneously try to assign a numerical value to that chance, which simply confuses risk with probability. In the markets we are talking about unique, nonrepeatable events, so we can't assign a frequency probability to their occurrence. In statistical terminology, such events are categorized under case probability, not class probability. This means the probability of market events is not open to any kind of numerical evaluation. All you can actually determine is the amount of your exposure as opposed to the probability that the market will or will not go to a certain price. Therefore, all you can do is manage your exposure and losses, not predict profits.

Money Odds vs. Probability Odds

Perhaps the most common fallacy to which market participants are susceptible is money odds vs. probability odds. Many market participants express the probability of success in terms of a risk-reward ratio. For example, if I bought my famous takeover stock (which you will hear about in the next chapter) at twenty-six dollars and placed a sell stop below the market at twenty-three dollars with an upside objective of thirty-six dollars, my risk-reward ratio would be three to ten. Risk three dollars to make ten dollars. It is clear that I don't understand probability. Couching my rationalizations in arithmetic terms does not automatically lend credibility to my position. The three-to-ten ratio has nothing to do with the *probability* that the stock can or will get to thirty-six dollars. All the ratio does is compare the dollar amount of what *I think I might lose* to the dollar amount of what *I think I might make*. But it doesn't say anything about the probability of either event occurring.

Some Dollars Are Bigger Than Others

Why did the dollars seem so big at the blackjack table? Because I was accustomed to dealing with price ticks in the market, not tokens with $25 or $100 printed on them. Ordinarily, the use of chips is a psychological gimmick to minimize the importance of money, and it works on most people. But I was used to handling hundreds of thousands of dollars of market transactions on the simple shout of my voice, which made it seem like money wasn't actually involved. When I had to physically take two twenty-five-dollar chips and throw them on the blackjack table, it felt like real money.

Being down $2,000 in ticks in the market doesn't feel the same as being down $2,000 at that baccarat table. It hurt a lot in baccarat. Also, the $7,000 in baccarat winnings felt like a lot more money than $7,000 in the market. Why? In the pit I was supposed to be working to try to make that kind of money, but in baccarat it was like free money. That means spending the $7,000 won in the casino was a lot easier than spending money made in the markets. The night after we'd won all the money, Conrad, Broderick, and I met a broker friend of Conrad's who was trying to get some of Conrad's business. We wanted to go to the best restaurant in town. The broker swore we wouldn't be able to get a table on such short notice and without a reservation. Well, we went to the restaurant anyway and I slipped the maitre d' hundred-dollar bills until he got us a table. It cost $600 but it was worth it to upstage the other broker. The money wasn't important because we hadn't worked for it. Those hundred-dollar bills were not nearly as big as the ones I had to work for in the pit.

PROFIT MOTIVE OR PROPHET MOTIVE?

There are two kinds of reward in the world: recognition and money. Are you in the market for recognition, congratulating yourself for calling every market move ahead of time and explaining the move after the fact, or are you in the market to make money? Are you more interested in the psychological reward of gold stars than the financial reward of gold coins? Are you trying to be right or to make money? Are you motivated by the prophet motive or the profit motive? To answer, you have to figure out which type of participant you are: bettor, gambler, investor, trader, or speculator. You do this by examining the *characteristics* and *behaviors* you are exhibiting, not the activity, i.e., opining on the outcome of a political race, playing at a blackjack table, buying stocks, trading in the pit, or buying/selling commodity futures from your Blue Bird Wanderlodge. The characteristics displayed determine the activity.

Embarking upon games or entering the markets can be either an end or a means.[5] It is an *end* for people who yearn for the stimulation and excitement that the vicissitudes of a game or the market provide them (e.g., gamblers) or those whose vanity is flattered by the display of their superiority in playing a game that requires cunning and skill (e.g., bettors). It is a means for professionals who want to make money (e.g., speculators, investors, and traders).

One morning Joe Siegel and I were on the trading floor when one of my accounts called in from vacation.

"What's lumber doing today?"

"It's limit up."

"Why?"

"The cash market is a lot stronger because storms in the Northwest are making it hard to get the lumber out from the mills."

"Where's cash?"

I told him prices for two-by-fours of white fir, western SPF, and green Douglas fir, and continued reading the news wire. The "green" in green Douglas fir refers to the fact that it has been newly cut (it has not been dried), just like someone who is new at something is referred to as green.

Siegel looked over at me and said, "I never have understood why they get such a premium price for lumber that they paint green."

I couldn't believe it. Here was Joe Siegel, easily trading more lumber futures than anyone else on the floor, and he didn't even know the difference between green and kiln-dried lumber in the cash market. I wasn't sure if he was kidding me or not. But looking back, I can only now see how it was possible for him to be such a successful trader without knowing that green lumber isn't actually painted green. He was a trader, and he relied on short-term information like order flow and price action to make his decisions because his time frame was short-term. He didn't let longer-term information more suited for investor types interfere with his trading. He knew the difference between traders and investors.

8

THE PSYCHOLOGICAL CROWD

Man is extremely uncomfortable with uncertainty. To deal with his discomfort, man tends to create a false sense of security by substituting certainty for uncertainty. It becomes the herd instinct.
—BENNETT W. GOODSPEED, *THE TAO JONES AVERAGES*

One day in the summer of 1980, *my partner Larry Broderick called me and said, "Hey, Jim, my stockbroker just called me with a tip, and we gotta buy this stock." Some company I can't even remember the name of (I told you I made investments that I couldn't remember) was a rumored takeover candidate. The broker said the "talk" was if the takeover happens, it would probably be within sixty days and probably at $60 a share. At the time, the stock was at trading $25.*

So we checked to see if there were options on the stock. The 35 strike calls were trading way out of the money and with very little time premium. They were trading for 1/16 or 1/8. You could buy thousands of these things for very little money. Well, we liked buying thousands of anything, so we bought thousands of these call options. And I did exactly the same thing I would do later in the bean oil; almost everybody I knew had to have a couple of hundred of these options. Among all of our clients and acquaintances, we had tens of thousands of the 35 strike calls. I'd call my futures customers and say, "Look, I can't sell you this stuff but trust me, go call your stockbroker and buy some." Now, who's not going to believe me when I tell them to buy something I can't even sell them or make any money on? They believe!

So, they bought the options. They all bought them. Everybody we knew bought them. Then the stock started to move, $25 ... $26 ... $27 ... $28 ... $29 ..., and volume started picking up, too. Pretty soon the options started *moving even though they were still trading for less than $1. When an option goes from 1/16 to 3/4, if you own 2,000 or 3,000 of them, you're talking some serious money. I had control of 300,000 shares at $35. At the $60 takeover price that's a $7,500,000 profit.*

Naturally, once something starts to work it's real easy to get people to believe you. "Okay, I told you to buy these options two weeks ago when they were at 1/16. Now they are at 3/4. Do you want to get in or do you want to stay stupid?" If I knew you, you had to have at least of couple of hundred of these things just for health insurance. What do I mean by health insurance? If I tell you that something which costs 1/16 today might be worth $25 inside of one month, you have to buy some of it. It's health insurance because once I tell you a story like that and you don't buy some and it happens, you're going to kill yourself. That's health insurance.

In three weeks the stock was up to $37 or $38 and our options were in the money. We had paid 1/16 for them and now they were worth $3 or $4. Then one Friday afternoon after the futures markets had closed, we were all up in my office and I was holding court. The phone rang. It was my partner, Larry. "Holy shit! They just stopped trading in our stock, Jim! News to follow!"

"That's it! That's it!" I screamed. "It's done. Holy . . . it's done."

They had ceased trading in "our stock"—news pending. Somebody was going to pay $60 for this stock that we owned at $35. We went home for the weekend thinking that Monday morning we were going to be millionaires. One of our biggest customers had 10,000 or 15,000 of these options, and he called British Airways to find out what it would cost to rent the Concorde— just for us! He actually wanted to lease the Concorde and fly to London to celebrate. We were all going to meet in New York at the Waldorf-Astoria, get on the Concorde and go to London and have a good time. I don't remember the exact figure, but the rental would have been like $200,000 or $300,000. That kind of money wouldn't have been a problem considering that we were all going to be multimillionaires come Monday morning.

Well, Monday morning the stock was still under the news pending restriction, but the options opened and they were higher. After about half an hour, the stock finally opened—down $6! The news that came out was "the pending, potential buyout" had been killed. Our options expired worthless. But for a weekend, I thought I was going to be a real six-million-dollar man.

EMOTIONS AND THE CROWD

Perhaps the most frequently cited reason for losses in the markets is emotion. These explanations run the gamut from simply citing greed and fear to others that go into great detail on emotions, their source from early childhood, and their effect on you. But examining individual emotions misses the point. Emotions are neither good nor bad; they simply are. They cannot be avoided. But emotionalism (i.e., decision making based on emotions) is bad, can be controlled, and should be avoided. So instead of examining each of the many individual emotions, this chapter will focus on the entity that epitomizes emotionalism: the crowd.

Emotions are very strong feelings arising subjectively rather than through *conscious* mental effort. As will be shown shortly, the fundamental characteristic of a crowd is that it is exclusively guided by *unconscious* motives. In other words, it is guided by emotions. If you don't have conscious control of your actions, then your emotions have control of you. Therefore, in order to understand how emotionalism adversely affects you as an investor, trader, or speculator, you have to know the characteristics and behaviors of the crowd. The nineteenth-century philosopher Gustave Le Bon put it this way: "Crowds are somewhat like the sphinx of ancient fable: it is necessary to arrive at a solution to the problem offered by their psychology or resign ourselves to being devoured by them."[1]

CONVENTIONAL VIEWS OF THE CROWD

1. Runaway Markets

All of us are familiar with the old market sayings about the public and the crowd such as: "Don't follow the crowd," "Be contrarian," "Trade opposite the general public." But most people don't really know what a crowd is, much less how to recognize it, and still less whether they are a part of the crowd. Most explanations of the crowd are actually studies of, or references to, the investing frenzies that have gripped mankind throughout history. For example, in his 1841 book *Extraordinary Popular Delusions and the Madness of Crowds*, British historian Charles Mackay recounts, among other manias, one of the more famous times in history when the crowd lost its collective head: Holland's tulip mania. In 1634 a speculative boom in Holland's primitive stock market spilled over into the flower marts, similar to the manner in which the speculative boom in the world stock markets in the 1980s spilled over into the art market. People in all stations of life converted their property into cash and invested it in tulip bulbs. At the peak of the tulip market in February 1637, single bulbs sold for prices equal to ten years' wages of the average worker.

Looking at such historical speculative episodes in search of common patterns has produced various models that describe the stages of the process at work when a market is driven by a crowd. For instance, in *Manias, Panics, and Crashes* by Charles P. Kindleberger we find the Minsky Model: (1) Displacement—some exogenous event (war, crop failure, etc.) shocks the macroeconomic system. (2) Opportunities—the displacement creates profitable opportunities in some sectors of the economy and closes down other sectors. Investment and production focuses on the profitable sectors and a boom is underway. (3) Credit expansion—an expansion of credit feeds the boom. (4) Euphoria—speculation for price increases couples with investment for production/sale.[2]

Another common pattern used to describe the crowd overtaking a market is (1) speculation, (2) credit expansion, (3) financial distress, (4) crisis, (5) panic and crash.

There are variations on these models, but essentially the crowd has been studied, described, and explained in terms of historical events rather than as a mental process that can happen to individuals. Thus, the crowd is seen as some kind of anonymous *they* who got caught up in a runaway market.

2. Contrarian Approach

Another way of viewing the crowd is the contrarian approach to the market, in which people look for universal endorsement at market tops and capitulation at market bottoms. Contrarians take market positions opposite the crowd. But you can't always be positioned opposite the crowd. In fact, you probably will be positioned the same way as the crowd at least some of the time because it's the only way your idea can become profitable; the crowd must come in and move the market the way you were positioned for it to go.

These conventional views of the crowd do not serve our purpose. Knowing the patterns of manias, panics, and crashes may be helpful in recognizing when such episodes are beginning to repeat themselves in the market, but these patterns reveal little about an individual's decision-making process. The patterns describe market events, not the mental state of an individual forming part of a crowd. Since our focus is on market participants rather than historians or economists, we don't need models to warn us of impending manias or panics in a market. Rather, we need a model to alert us to when we are becoming part of a crowd.

WHAT IS A CROWD?

In the ordinary sense, the word *crowd* means a gathering of individuals regardless of what has brought them together. But according to Le Bon, in his book *The Crowd*, from a psychological perspective the word means something entirely different. When the sentiments and ideas of all the people in the gathering take one and the same direction and their conscious individual personality disappears, then the gathering has become a *psychological crowd*.[3] It is my contention that this process does not require a gathering of people; an isolated individual who displays those characteristics is, for all intents and purposes, a member of the crowd.

Can you be classified as part of the crowd even if you're sitting alone in your den following the markets? Yes—if you're wavering back and forth like a candle in the wind, swayed by every news story or price change on the screen. Are you displaying the characteristics of a crowd in your individual decision-making process? If you are evidencing the tendencies, emotions, and characteristics of the crowd in your actions and reactions to the market, then you are making a *crowd trade.*

The basic distinction between the individual and the crowd is that the individual acts after reasoning, deliberation, and analysis; a crowd acts on feeling, emotion, and impulses. An individual will think out his opinions whereas a crowd is swayed by emotional viewpoints rather than by reasoning. In the crowd, emotional and thoughtless opinions spread widely via imitation and contagion.[4] Learning the characteristics of a crowd and how it forms will provide a structure that shows how emotionalism affects your decision making. Once you know the structure, you'll know what to avoid in order to prevent emotionalism.

CHARACTERISTICS OF A CROWD

There are three main characteristics that describe the mental state of an individual forming a part of a crowd. As you will see, the same characteristics can also be exhibited by an individual making investment and trading decisions.

1. A Sentiment of Invincible Power

The individual forming part of a crowd acquires a sentiment of invincible power; the improbable doesn't exist for the crowd or its members. According to *Webster's* dictionary, *sentiment* is a complex combination of feelings and opinions as a basis for judgment. This feeling of invincible power tends to make a person yield to instincts and emotions that he would ordinarily keep in check. But the crowd is anonymous, and anyone in the crowd will shirk responsibility for his actions. In a crowd people do things they wouldn't ordinarily do because they are anonymous and feed off the power provided by the crowd. The responsibility that keeps individuals in control vanishes in the crowd. (Witness the actions of fans who storm the football field after a victory and tear down the goal posts.) This is how I was in the bean-oil trade. I was invincible. I could do no wrong. As far as I was concerned, there was no question that the trade was going to make $10 million.

2. Contagion

The American Heritage Dictionary defines *contagion* as the tendency to spread as an influence or emotional state. This is like the spontaneous wave at a football stadium or the riots that break out in a city after a home team's championship victory. It's like being hypnotized or mesmerized. Watching prices change on the computer screen, getting quotes from your broker throughout the day, seeing the stock ticker on the bottom of your TV screen, or just being in the market and experiencing prices going up and down can serve as the hypnotist's watch swinging back and forth in front of his subject. This describes my mental state in the motor home when I was keeping up with the markets on the telephone.

3. Suggestibility

The best way to describe this is the way a hypnotized subject, in the hands of his hypnotizer, responds to the power of suggestion. He is highly suggestible and no longer conscious of his acts. Under the influence of a suggestion, he will undertake the accomplishment of certain acts with irresistible impetuosity. This sounds just like me when I was driving down the Jersey Turnpike, glued to my telephone and listening to the changing prices, and when I took the suggestions on the bean oil-trade and the stock trades and ran with them. In the special state of fascination (contagion), an individual is in the hands of the price changes on the screen, the words and suggestions of whoever got him into the market in the first place, or anyone else from whom he seeks opinions.

The most striking peculiarity presented by a psychological crowd is the following: Once individuals have formed a crowd, however like or unlike their mode of life, their occupation, their character, or their intelligence, that fact that they have been transformed into a crowd puts them in possession of a sort of collective mind that makes them act in a manner quite different from that in which each individual would act, were he in a state of isolation.[5] A person in a crowd also allows himself to be induced to commit acts contrary to his most obvious interests. One of the most incomprehensible features of a crowd is the tenacity with which the members adhere to erroneous assumptions despite mounting evidence to challenge them. [6] So when an individual adheres to a market position despite the mounting losses, he is a crowd.

These observations explain what happens when you do something you said you weren't going to do or fail to do something you said you would do. They also explain why I stayed in bean oil after I began losing more than I ever had made in the position. It was obviously not in my best interest to take money from other ventures and borrow money to pay for the losses that were accumulating. Why would I let a once-profitable position go to the point where I actually had to borrow money to stay in the position? If you had posed that possibility to me in 1973 or 1976, or even in August 1983, I would have completely rejected the notion that I could ever do such a thing. If you have ever had a position on and intended to do one thing but actually did something else, then you were a member of the psychological crowd and made a *crowd trade*—whether you knew it or not. Otherwise, you would have done what you originally intended.

The point is that in addition to the traditional views of the crowd in the markets, there is also such thing as a crowd investment or a crowd trade that an individual can make, even without the presence or influence of other people. The similarities between a psychological crowd and a losing market participant are striking. Remember, it is not a function of a quantity of individuals that determines if a psychological crowd has formed. Rather, it is a function of the characteristics displayed. If a person is exhibiting these characteristics, then he is part of a psychological crowd and is making *crowd trades*.

The market doesn't even have to be frothy for an individual to make a crowd trade, nor does it have to fall into either of the crowd models described earlier. The market can just be going sideways, and he can still be making a crowd trade, if he is exhibiting the special characteristics of crowds such as impulsiveness, irritability, incapacity to reason, exaggeration of sentiments, absence of critical judgment, etc. If this isn't the profile of an emotional (and losing) market participant, then nothing is. It describes me perfectly when I was in the bean-oil trade and the takeover-stock trade, not to mention many other trades.

The two models below are adapted from Le Bon's book *The Crowd*. While he was interested in the processes and characteristics of mob behavior from a sociological point of view, we are interested in how those processes and characteristics exhibit themselves in individuals making market decisions.

TWO PSYCHOLOGICAL CROWD MODELS

Delusion Model

The delusion model describes the process an individual becoming part of a psychological crowd *before* he has a position on.

(1) Expectant Attention (2) Suggestion Made (3) Process of Contagion (4) Acceptance by All Present.

This model illustrates exactly how the net loser participates in the markets. He is ready! Because he is so anxious to make money, he is in a state of expectant attention. He hears a tip or a casual comment about the market; enthusiasm is contagious and he goes into a hypnotic-like trance, takes the tip as gospel, and acts on it. Compare this to when you've made hasty, impulsive, spur-of-the-moment decisions or followed someone else's tip to get in or out of the market. I went through the same process when I entered the takeover-stock trade and the bean-oil position. In both of these instances, as well as many others, I was in an expectant state of attention, ready to make money. Once the trades were suggested to me, a process of contagion took over, and I acted.

The reason people who try to make back losses quickly lose again is because they are in an expectant state of attention ready to pounce on any trade suggested. This makes them part of the crowd, emotional to the extreme, and bound to lose.

The Illusion Model

The illusion model accurately describes the process of an individual becoming part of a psychological crowd *after* he has a position on.

(1) Affirmation (2) Repetition (3) Prestige (4) Contagion

Consider the following scenario. An opinion about the market is expressed (affirmation) either by you or someone else. It gets repeated (repetition) to others. Friends ask what you think about the markets, and you repeat the opinion, selling yourself on the idea once again. Next, prestige comes into play. Prestige is a sort of domination exercised over us by an individual, a work, an idea, or a wish. It entirely paralyzes our critical faculty and fills us with wonderment. The market is going your way; you look like a hero; you're so smart (prestige); you have the adulation of your peers. Emotionalism overwhelms you (contagion). You're hypnotized.

The illusion model can also be applied to losing trades if the prestige involved comes from your daring actions and being able to take the punishment of a losing position. Sure, the market is against you, but you're courageous and you can take it. The market is wrong and will turn around. You take pride in your courage to go against the crowd because, according to market lore, the crowd is supposed to be wrong. People marvel at your ability to stay with a losing position. Once again, you become hypnotized (contagion) and are out of control. The trade will end only when you are forced out by external forces (e.g., money, family, margin clerk). This is exactly what I did once the bean-oil position started going against me. Why else would I let the once profitable bean-oil position erode to the point where I'd basically lost my prior life?

EMOTIONS

Recall from basic economics that markets exist to satisfy the *wants* and *needs* of consumers. This means people make purchases for only one of two reasons: *to feel better* (satisfying a want) or to *solve a problem* (satisfying a need). Trying to do the former in the financial markets is dangerous. If you are in the markets to achieve a certain emotional state or create self-esteem, then you have some psychological disorders and need to see a therapist. Just as compulsive gambling, which is a personality disorder, isn't the focus of this book, neither are the other psychological pathologies. Our discussion only addresses the normal emotional ups and downs of participating in the markets, not the psychological disorders. Remember, emotions per se are neither good nor bad; they just are. It's emotionalism we are trying to avoid.

HOPE/FEAR PARADOX

Psychologists and psychiatrists usually advise against suppressing emotions, and suppression usually involves negative emotions. Rarely, if ever, are patients treated for suppressing positive emotions. Surprising as it may sound, however, both positive and negative emotions can have detrimental effects on your decisions and performance in the markets. To see why this is true, let's examine the ailments of hope and fear and their unique link to the crowd.

Ordinarily, greed and fear are cited as the two driving emotions of market participants. However, hope and fear are the primary emotions; greed is simply hope run amok. The advice on hope and fear is almost as conflicting as the advice the pros give us on making money. We have all been told not to buy/sell a stock or make a trade based on hope or fear: never hope that a position will go our way and never fear that a position won't go our way. We've been told that hope causes us to buy a stock after it has already gone up and we buy it at the top; fear causes us to sell a stock after it has already gone down a lot and we wind up selling at the bottom. Or in the words of the father of contrary thinking, Humphrey Neil, "The crowd is most enthusiastic and optimistic when it should be cautious and prudent, and it is most fearful when it should be bold."[7] On the other hand, we read Jesse Livermore's advice that we should hope when we would fear and fear when we would hope. That is, we should hope our profits will become bigger profits instead of fearing the profits will turn around, and we should fear our losses will become bigger losses instead of hoping the losses will turn around.

The conflicting advice is explained by the paradox that hope and fear are merely two sides of the same coin. In other words, more often than not you are likely to experience both hope and fear simultaneously.

When you're long and the market is going up, you

(1) hope it will keep going but
(2) fear it won't.

If your fear is great enough, you will get out and hope the market turns down.

When you're long and the market goes down, you

(1) hope it will turn around but
(2) fear it won't.

If your fear is great enough, you'll get out and hope that it keeps going down.

When you're *not* long in the market but want to be and the market goes up, you

(1) hope it will temporarily turn around to let you in but
(2) fear it will keep going.

If your fear is great enough, you will buy and hope the market keeps going up.

The point is: focusing on individual emotions can be quite confusing, and it is better to focus on emotionalism instead. The best way to do that is by understanding the psychological crowd.

MANIA AND PANIC: WHERE HOPE AND FEAR MEET THE CROWD

As the epigraph to this chapter states, man is extremely uncomfortable with uncertainty, tries to substitute certainty for uncertainty, and, in doing so, succumbs to the herd instinct. That uncertainty about the future also elicits two primary emotional responses: hope and fear. We hope the future will turn out well, but we fear it won't. As members of the crowd we will always take these emotions to extremes. When the herd instinct combines with hope and fear in a market environment, we get panics and manias.

According to *The American Heritage Dictionary*, a *mania* is an inordinately intense enthusiasm or hope for something; a craze, a fad, or a behavior that enjoys brief popularity and pertains to the common people or people at large. It defines a *panic* as a sudden, overpowering terror often affecting many people at once. (It also says to see the synonym, *fear.*) Notice that the definitions of both *mania* and *panic* have direct references to *hope* and *fear* and the *crowd*.

Manias and panics don't have to be full-scale mass population events like the tulips in Holland; they can occur on the scale of an individual making decisions about entering and exiting the market. Since an isolated individual can be classified as a crowd, then the same individual can get involved in a solitary panic or mania. And the market doesn't even have to be frothy for this to happen. It can be going sideways, and the individual can experience a solitary panic or mania simply by exhibiting the characteristics of a crowd coupled with hope or fear.

In a solitary panic, crowd behavior combines with an individual's fear of losing money or fear of missing an opportunity to profit and becomes the primary reason for acting or failing to act. In a solitary mania, crowd behavior combines with an individual's intense hope for profit or hope that a losing position will turn around and becomes the primary reason for acting or failing to act.

So instead of trying to monitor yourself for all the different emotions and what they might mean, simply monitor yourself for the few stages of crowd formation. By avoiding the tell-tale symptoms that accompany becoming part of the crowd, you will automatically avoid emotionalism.

The day after my $248,000 Thursday in August of 1983, Broderick and I were sitting on the dock at his lake house. He turned to me and said, "What's the only thing that can keep this market from really going?" I thought a minute and said, "Well . . . if it rains that'll change things."

That night we were watching the news, and the weather report called for rain over the weekend. Broderick looked at me and said, "Well? That's it, right?" I said, "Well . . . no . . . it ain't . . . it may not be enough rain . . . and it's not really getting Indiana . . ." It only took me about half an hour to decide that the rain didn't matter. There wasn't enough rain in the right places, and the market had already shrugged off that little bit of rain by closing higher that day.

Broderick got out of the market on Monday—because it had rained. And I had told him that if it rained the trade was over. So he got out and he made money. But me? No! I had to stick and stay and tell myself it hadn't rained enough. I was not going to be tricked out of one of the best trades of the decade by "a little rain." I had my own solitary mania going on.

To repeat the leitmotiv of the book thus far: people lose (really lose, not just have occasional losing trades) because of psychological factors, not analytical ones (chapter 5). They personalize the market and their positions (chapters 1 through 4), internalizing what should be external losses (chapter 6), confusing the different types of risk activities (chapter 7), and making crowd trades (chapter 8). Is there a single factor common to all of these errors, and can we determine a way to address that factor in order to avoid the errors?

PART THREE

TYING IT ALL TOGETHER

9

RULES, TOOLS, AND FOOLS

A fool must now and then be right by chance.

—WILLIAM COWPER

The final irony of this story is that the bean-oil market turned shortly after I blew out in November 1983. If I had been able to stay in the market a little longer, by May 1984 my 540 spreads would have been worth $3,200,000. In hindsight, however, I don't think it would have made any difference. Sooner or later I was going to lose all of my money, and the later it was, the more I was going to lose. If I had ridden through that valley of death and come out the other side with $3,200,000, somewhere along the line, in some other trade, I would have ended up losing $6,000,000 instead of $1,600,000. It just would have postponed the inevitable loss and made it bigger. Is it possible that I might have done some smart things like pay off the house or lock some money away? Maybe. But I still believe that eventually the disaster was going to happen.

Why am I so sure it was inevitable? Because even though I had succeeded in many things in life by treating them like games and simply following the rules (i.e., freshman English, the MSV test, OCS, and the honor graduate award), I had also succeeded in many other things by breaking the rules. A lot of things I did worked but shouldn't have. For instance, nobody calls a frat house during rush, asks for a pledge pin, and gets it. Nobody gets elected to the Board of Governors of the Chicago Mercantile Exchange because he wears $600 suits, $50 ties, and Bally shoes. Once I realized I was *breaking the rules but still succeeding, I thought rules were for everybody else and that I could break them and still succeed.*

What this means is that sometimes I was breaking the rules whether I knew it or not, and that one time I was going to be wrong (and we will all be wrong sometimes) but not accept or believe it. That approach ensured that when the loss occurred, it would wipe me out.

If you occasionally break the rules and still have an unbroken string of successes, you are likely to compound the problem because you assume that you are better than other people and above the rules. Your ego inflates, and you refuse to recognize the reality of a loss when it comes. You assume that you will be right. You assume that even if the market is against you, it will come back. Well, if I had an ego problem at one million dollars, what kind of problem would I have had if I had ridden through the valley of death and cheated death? If I had survived the loss and the market had gone on to make money for me, my ego problem would have been much worse.

TYING IT ALL TOGETHER

To answer the question posed at the end of the last chapter—Yes, there is a common factor that triggers the mental processes, behavioral characteristics, and emotions of a net loser: the uncertainty of the future. In a certain world we wouldn't have to choose or act. Certainty would replace probability. We wouldn't have the *potential for loss* (i.e., risk). and, therefore, we wouldn't have any risk activities, created or inherent. We would neither have losses nor experience the Five Stages of Internal Loss. In the words of financial editor James Grant, "Because the future is always unfathomable, there are always buyers and sellers in every market. If the socialists were right—if the future could be accurately divined—markets would disband because nobody would ever take the losing side of a trade."[1] Since the herd instinct and crowd behavior arise out of our desire to replace uncertainty with certainty, if the future were certain we wouldn't succumb to emotionalism. Likewise, hope and fear, which are our strongest emotional responses to the uncertain future, wouldn't subject us to personal panics and manias. As it happens, we don't live in a certain world, so we need a way to deal with the uncertain future.

DEALING WITH THE UNCERTAINTY OF THE FUTURE

All enterprise, all human activity inextricably involves risk for the simple reason that the future is never certain, never completely revealed to us.[2] When dealing with the risk of the uncertainty of the future, you have three choices: engineering, gambling, or speculating. The engineer knows everything he needs to know for a technologically satisfactory answer to his problems. He builds safety margins into his calculations to eliminate any fringes of uncertainty. Therefore, the engineer basically operates in a world of certainty since he knows and controls most, if not all, of the variables which affect the outcome of his work.[3] The gambler, on the other hand, knows nothing about the event on which the outcome of his gambling depends because the distinguishing feature of gambling is that it deals with the unknown. The gambler plays for the excitement— the adrenaline rush. He isn't playing to win—he is just playing.[4] The speculator doesn't have the advantage of the engineer. The rules of natural science will not render the future direction of prices predictable. But the speculator does know more than the gambler because while the gambler is dealing with pure chance, the speculator has at least some knowledge about what determines the outcome of his activity. Speculating is the application of intellectual examination and systematic analysis to the problem of the uncertain future.

Successful investing is the result of successful speculation. If your "investment" is a stock, you are depending on the managers of the firm to accurately foresee the market for the goods it produces. If your investment is a bank savings account, you are depending on the loan officers at the bank to accurately foresee future business conditions and make prudent, profitable loans that generate the interest the bank pays to you. Interest doesn't just materialize out of thin air simply by putting money in the bank. (This is a reference to banking the way it used to be, ignoring FDIC insurance in order to make a point.) Federal Reserve Chairman Alan Greenspan put it this way: "The historic purpose of banking is to take prudent risks through the extension of loans to risk taking businesses."[5] In other words, the bankers are speculating.

Successful trading is also the result of successful speculation. The trader has a methodical approach to bidding and offering stock (or bonds, futures, currencies, etc.) and monitoring market conditions for any subtle changes in supply and demand. He knows only too well the perils of predicting and doesn't try to forecast market direction. He operates under strict parameters of "if . . . then" statements that dictate his subsequent buy and sell decisions.

Successful hedging, too, is a function of successful speculation. The hedger examines current and prospective business and market conditions, and he speculates as to how they might change and whether he can turn a profit at today's prices. If so, he hedges his inventory or inventory needs.

Speculation is forethought. And thought before action implies reasoning before a decision is made about what, whether, and when to buy or sell. That means the speculator develops several possible scenarios of future events and determines what his actions will be under each scenario. He thinks before he acts. The sequence of thinking before acting is the exact definition of the word *plan*. Therefore, speculating and planning are the same thing. A plan allows you to speculate with a long time horizon (as an investor), a short time horizon (as a trader), or on a spread relationship (as a basis trader or hedger). Since you can't really be an engineer in the market (unless you're a "rocket scientist" on Wall Street) and since we've already discussed the dangers of gambling in the markets, then speculating, and therefore having a plan, is the only way to deal with the uncertainty of the future in the markets. Given this definition, for the remainder of the book Speculator (capitalized) will be used to include investors, speculators, and traders, all of whom are Speculating.

A *plan*, the noun, is a detailed scheme, program, or method worked out beforehand for the accomplishment of an objective. *To plan*, the verb, means to think before acting, not to think and act simultaneously nor to act before thinking. Without a plan, you fall into one of two categories: a bettor, if your main concern in being right, or a gambler, if your main concern is entertainment. If you express an opinion on what the market will do, you've gotten yourself personally involved with the market. You start to regard what the market does as a personal reflection. You feel vindicated if price moves in the direction you predicted and wrong if it doesn't. Moreover, when the market moves against you, you feel obligated to say something to justify your opinion, or, worse, you feel obligated to do something like show the courage of your conviction by adding to a losing position. Participating to be right is betting, and betting for excitement is gambling. In order to be speculating, by definition you must have a plan.

DECISION MAKING

As we saw in chapter 6, participating in the markets is about decision making. You must decide the conditions under which you will enter the market before developing a plan to implement the decision. Obviously, if you decide not to enter the market there is no need for a plan. Broadly speaking, the decision-making process is as follows: (1) Decide what type of participant you're going to be, (2) select a method of analysis, (3) develop rules, (4) establish controls, and (5) formulate a plan. Depending on what your goals or objectives are on the continuum of conservative to aggressive, you will decide whether you are an investor or speculator, which in turn will help you decide what markets to participate in, what method of analysis you'll use, what rules you'll develop, what controls you'll have, and how you will implement these things with a plan. We already know that no single analytical method will be successful for everyone. Instead, you are likely to find some type of method that is compatible with your tolerance for exposure. You will fill in the specifics based on your research and your tolerance for exposure.

The first thing you decide is what type of participant you are going to be (investor or speculator). Then you select what market you are going to participate in (stocks, bonds, currencies, futures). The plan you develop must be consistent with the characteristics and time horizon of the type of participant you choose to be. Why? Changing your initial time horizon in the middle of a trade changes the type of participant you are and is almost as dangerous as betting or gambling in the market. For example, what's an investment to most people who dabble in the stock market? Ninety percent of the time an "investment" is a "trade" that didn't work. People start with the idea of making money in a relatively short period of time, but when they start losing money they lengthen their time frame horizon and suddenly the trade becomes an investment. "I really think you ought to buy XYZ here, Jim. It's trading at $20, and it's going to $30." We buy and it goes down to $15. "It's really a good deal here at $15. It's gonna be fine." So we buy more. Then it goes to $10. "Okay, we're taking the long term view. That's an investment." How many shares of Penn Central are in trust funds in this country? Lots. Because they invested in the great American railroad. When it went from $86 in 1968 to $6 in 1970, in their minds they couldn't sell it because they had lost too much. So they lengthened their time frame in order to rationalize hanging on to the losing position. Or how about IBM, the darling of institutional and individual investors alike? Its stock went from $175 in 1987 to $45 in 1993 with buy recommendations from analysts all the way down.

One of the problems most stock players face is that they buy the stock because of a fundamental story. They believe a story just like I believed the bean-oil story: "We're going to run out of bean oil. There's going to be a shortage and people will pay up." If I buy a stock because I think earnings are going to be up but then the stock starts down, I've got a problem. As a stock player who believed the story, I have to decide: "Either I'm stupid to have believed it in the first place, or the market is wrong." Which do you think I'm going to pick? The market is wrong, of course. So I fight the market, hold the losing position, and turn my trade into an investment.

Consider the following story about an individual investor reported by the *Wall Street Journal*: "After seeing the nearly 87% return that Twentieth Century Investor's Ultra Fund racked up in 1991 by concentrating on biotech and computer-related stocks, he took the plunge, paying about $18 a share for the Ultra fund. A year later with Ultra shares below $15 a share he felt stuck. 'Some people say cut your losses, but I've already lost too much,' the investor said. 'Luckily, I don't need the money right away.'" Well, is the market going to conveniently rebound for him when he does need the money? "I can't get out here, I'm losing too much," is the worst thing you'll hear a trader or investor say! What he is saying is: he's getting absolutely crushed, crucified, and buried, and he can't get out of the market *because* he's getting crushed, crucified, and buried. That's stupid. Anytime someone says he can't get out because he's losing too much, he has personalized the market; he just doesn't want to lose face by realizing the loss. To make matters worse, since most stock players pay for their stock in full, they are very prone to extending their original time horizon. Why? Because they are never forced out of the market when the position starts to lose money. Even when they buy stocks on margin, it's a 50 percent margin as opposed to normal 4 percent to 12 percent for futures traders. So it's very easy in the stock market to let a loss get out of control simply by lengthening your time horizon and becoming an investor.

The stock investor *can* stay in the position forever. A futures speculator, on the other hand, will be forced out of the market when the contract expires. So even if he has financed a losing futures position, he is forced into making a new decision at expiration as to whether to stay with the position. The stock player has no such forcing point, which is why it's especially important to decide what type of participant you're going to be when you're in the stock market.

Next, you must select a method of market analysis that you are going to use. Otherwise, you will jump back and forth among several methods in search of supporting evidence to justify holding onto a market position. Because there are so many ways to analyze the market, you will inevitably find some indicator from some method of analysis that can be used to justify holding a position. This is true for both profitable and unprofitable positions: you will keep a profitable position longer than originally intended and possibly have it turn into a loss, and you will rationalize holding a losing position far beyond what you were originally willing to lose.

Your analysis is the set of tools you will use to describe market conditions. Fundamental analysis in the stock market doesn't tell you when to enter the market. There isn't a magic formula combining the various fundamental data that tells you when to buy and when to sell. A certain level of expected earnings combined with its P/E ratio, price-to-book-value ratio, and other fundamental variables doesn't specifically instruct you on when to make actual purchases and sales. The different methods of technical analysis don't always offer specific instructions on when to make purchases or sales either. They are means of describing the conditions of the market. Analysis is simply that: analysis. It doesn't tell you what to do or when to do it.

In order to translate your analysis into something more than mere commentary, you need to define what constitutes an opportunity for you. That's what rules do; they implement your analysis. Rules are hard-and-fast. Tools (i.e., methods of analysis) have some flexibility in how they are used. Fools have neither rules nor tools. You must develop parameters that will define opportunities and determine how and when you will act. How? By doing homework (i.e., research, testing, trial and error) and defining the parameters with rules. Your homework determines what parameters or conditions define an opportunity, and your rules are the "if . . . then" statements that implement your analysis. This means entry and exit points are derived after you have done your analysis.

If the opportunity-defining criteria aren't met, you don't act. This doesn't mean a particular trade or investment that you pass up won't turn out to be profitable. It might have been an acceptable and profitable trade based on someone else's rules. Remember, participating in the markets is about making decisions, and as Drucker reminds us, "There is no perfect decision. One always has to pay a price which might mean passing up an opportunity."[6] You have to accept the fact that profitable situations will occur that you won't participate in. Don't worry about the ones you miss; they were someone else's. Your rules will only enable you to participate in some of the millions of possible opportunities, not all of them.

The next step in decision making is establishing controls, i.e., the exit criteria that will take you out of the market either at a profit or loss. They take the form of a price order, a time stop, or a condition stop (i.e., if a certain thing happens or fails to happen then you are getting out of the market). Your exit criteria create a discrete event, ending the position and preventing the continuous process from going on and on. According to Drucker, "controls follow strategy."[7] So in terms of a business plan, market selection and entry criteria constitute the strategy while exit criteria constitute controls. Drucker's observation means that the controls should be consistent with the strategy, not that they should be selected after the strategy is implemented. Unfortunately, most market participants pick their stop *after* they decide to enter the market and some never put in a stop at all. You must pick the loss side first. Why? Otherwise, after you enter the market everything you look at and hear will be skewed in favor of your position. For example, if someone has a long position and you ask him what he thinks about the market, is he going to tell you all the reasons why it should go down? Of course not. He's going to tell you all the reasons why it should go up. Another reason controls should precede strategy is that, as we learned in chapter 7, you can't calculate the probability of a trade's being profitable; you can only calculate your exposure. So all you can do is manage your losses, not predict profits.

THE PLAN

Eleven Herbs and Spices

Everyone wants to know the secret ingredients for a successful plan. However, it's not simply the individual ingredients that are important to know; it's the entire recipe: the set of instructions telling you in *what order* and in *what quantities* to mix the ingredients. Remember the old advertisements for Kentucky Fried Chicken? "The Colonel's secret blend of eleven herbs and spices." Well, Colonel Sanders could have safely told anyone the *names* of his eleven herbs and spices (i.e., the ingredients). As long as he didn't tell anyone the *secret blend* of his eleven herbs and spices (i.e., the measurements and the mixing instructions), he didn't have to worry about anybody stealing business from him.

No one can outline a plan that all market participants will accept. Besides, since there are so many different plans one can follow and be successful, it matters less *what* the plan is than it does that there is a plan. Remember, there are as many ways to make money in the markets as there are participants. There are also as many possible plans as there are participants, yet only one valid recipe for formulating a plan. Regardless of the methodology used, before you decide to get into the market you have to decide *where* (price) or *when* (time) or *why* (new information) you will no longer want the position.

Almost all commentary on the development of a plan will list the ingredients as entry, stop-loss, and price objective. However, to be effective as a loss-control tool, the plan *must* be derived by deciding STOP, ENTRY, then PRICE OBJECTIVE. Failure to choose a price objective could cost the trader some potential profits. A poor entry price could increase losses or reduce profits. But not having a predetermined stop-loss can, and ultimately will, cost you a lot of money. Usually, people pick the exit point after they enter the market—if they even bother to pick an exit point. Their exit point is a function of their entry point, and it's usually some arbitrary dollar amount that they are supposedly willing to lose. Then they rationalize it by expressing the trade in terms of the money odds fallacy—"It's a three-to-one risk-reward ratio! I'll risk $500 to make $1,500"—when there is no basis in statistical probability to support the assertion that the price will reach the profitable objective.

The distinguishing factor of "the" recipe is determining the stop-loss criteria before deciding *whether* and *where* to enter the market. Citing Drucker once again, "The first step in planning is to ask of any activity, any product, any process or market, 'If we were not committed to it today, would we go into it?' If the answer is no, one says, 'How can we get out—fast?' "[8] As a market participant you don't have to be committed to the market at all, so you ask the latter question before getting in the market in the first place. After you know where you want to get *out* of the market, then you can ascertain whether and where you are comfortable getting *into* the market. In contrast to what most people do, your entry point should be a function of the exit point. Once you specify what price or under what circumstances you would no longer want the position, and specify how much money you are willing to lose, then, and only then, can you start thinking about where to enter the market.

Naturally, this procedure will cause you to miss some good trades. Price-limit orders that were entered to initiate new positions yet remain unfilled are trades we wish had been made. However, "profitable trades" that are missed actually cost zero while poor controls (pick the stop later) or no controls (no stop) will sooner or later cost you a lot of money. Having picked your exit-loss criteria before entering the position, presumably you choose an amount of loss you could tolerate. After that, leave your exit order alone, change a trailing stop to lock in more profit if you're following a technical method of analysis, or monitor for any change in the fundamentals that you previously determined would cause you to exit the position if you're following a fundamental method. If you wait until after the position is established to choose your exit point or begin moving the stop to allow more room for losses or alter the fundamental factors you monitor in your decision making, then you (1) internalize the loss because you don't want to lose face, (2) bet or gamble on the position because you want to be right, and (3) make crowd trades because you're making emotional decisions. As a result, you will lose considerably more money than you can afford.

Your plan is a script of what you expect to happen based on your particular method of analysis and provides a clear course of action if it doesn't happen; you have prepared for different scenarios and know how you will react to each of them. This doesn't mean you're predicting the future. It means you know ahead of time what alternative courses of action you will take if event A, B, or C happens. The soundness of this approach for both markets and business is evidenced by something called scenario planning: "a structured, disciplined method for thinking about the future and a technique for anticipating developments in fluid political and economic situations."[9] The scenario technique was developed by strategists at the RAND Corporation to think through issues involving the nature of nuclear warfare. Analysts would posit possible outcomes and then identify how and what sequence of unexpected political events and economic trends would lead to each outcome. These would serve as signposts to watch for as the road to the future unfolded. In the early 1970s, planners at oil giant Royal Dutch Shell built on this technique and began applying it to the oil business. "The result was scenario planning which offered a way to evaluate strategy, test investment decisions—and clarify risk and uncertainty."[10] The oil industry operates on very long-term investments, the viability of which can be dramatically affected by social, economic, and technological changes. "As part of planning for the future, the Shell planners applied scenario planning not only to the energy business but also to larger global, economic, and social trends."[11] You, too, must use scenario analysis to clarify risk and uncertainty and plan for the future.

If you are using a technical-analysis approach to the market, the data you rely on to make decisions take one of two forms: either prices go up or they go down. If you are using a fundamental approach to the market, the events you rely on to make decisions can take many forms. But even with a fundamental method of analysis, you must have some amount of monetary loss that you deem intolerable. Remember, we are trying to manage possible scenarios and losses, not predict the future and profits. "Scenario planning does not, of course, tell us the future; only fortune-tellers can do that."[12] And we already know trying to predict means you're betting, which gets you all caught up in trying to be right. "The objective of the scenario approach is not to decide which scenario is right. . . . There is no 'right' answer."[13]

A preoccupation with wanting to be right or wanting to be perceived as being right, explains people's tendency to focus on *why* the market is doing what it is doing instead of *what* it is doing. They're constantly asking, "Why is the market up (or down)?" When someone asks, "Why is the market up?" does he really want to know why? No. If he is long he wants to hear the reason so he can reinforce his view that he is right, feel even better about it, and pat himself on the back. If he isn't long, he's probably short and wants to know why *the market* thinks the market is up, so that he can argue with it and convince himself that he is right and the market is wrong. He wants to say, "Oh, *that's* the reason? Well, that's the stupidest reason I ever heard." He wants to justify his position of being the "wrong" way in the market by asking "why" so he can say, "That's a stupid reason." Let me tell you some good news and some bad news about "why" and the markets. The good news is, if you're long and the market is going up and you don't have a clue as to why, you get to keep all the money. Every cent. They don't charge you a single penny if you were "only lucky." The bad news is, if the market is going up and you're short and you know exactly why it's up, you don't get any money back. Now how important is it to know *why*? Knowing *why* doesn't get you any brownie points with the market. Nor do you get any partial credit like you did in school for knowing *why* you got a math question wrong. And this is true for all business, not just the markets.

The *Wall Street Journal* had an article on John Kluge, once the richest man in America in the *Forbes* annual survey.[14] Just before Kluge bought the Ponderosa steakhouse chain in 1988 he met with some skeptical bankers who asked. "Don't you think this is the wrong business to be in?" Everyone in the country was talking about health food at the time, and steak wasn't on the list of food that was good for you. Kluge began pounding his fist on the table. "The people want steak," he shouted. He was so confident about the nation's appetite for T-bone and sirloin that he invested close to $1 billion in steak restaurants over the next three years. Lo and behold, although beef consumption was on the decline, steak sales at restaurants held steady.

"So Mr. Kluge was right: People do want steak. They just don't want his steak," the *Wall Street Journal* concluded.

But what good did it do for him to be right if he didn't make any money? Or even worse, lost money? Ponderosa was plagued by heavy losses, and Kluge had to pour money into the chain to keep it operating: $60 million in 1992 and another $30 million in 1993 to renovate 360 Ponderosas. The *Wall Street Journal* said that until that point, "Mr. Kluge had been known for his Midas touch." Sound familiar? I, too, thought I had the Midas touch. "There's going to be a shortage of bean oil!" And I was right; there was a shortage. But not only did I *not* make any money on it, I lost a lot. I poured money into that position from other ventures just to keep it going in a vain attempt to be *right*. And, like Kluge, I was right. But neither one of us made any money on the deals. So you can be *right* and lose money. But which is more important? Remember, there are two kinds of reward in the world: recognition and money. Are you being motivated by the prophet motive or the profit motive? In the markets and in business don't concern yourself with being right. Instead, follow your plan and watch the money.

Preoccupation with being right means you're betting, which personalizes the market and is the root of losses due to psychological factors. Concern yourself with whether you have done your homework to define a set of conditions under which you will enter and exit the market and whether you carry out that plan.

Now that we know what a real plan is, let's look at how having and following a plan addresses the uncertainty inherent in each of the areas covered in chapters 6, 7, and 8.

A PLAN VS. LOSS, RISK, AND THE CROWD

The uncertainty of the future when facing a market loss triggers the Five Stages of Internal Loss. Have you ever said to yourself, "No way! Is the market really down that far?" That's *denial*. Have you ever gotten mad at the market? Called it a name? Gotten angry at friends or family because of a position? That's *anger*. Ever begged the market or

God to get you back to breakeven so you could get out? That's *bargaining*. Has a market loss ever changed your sleep or diet patterns? That's *depression*. Ever have a firm liquidate one of your positions? That's *acceptance*. Unless you have a plan, your potential loss is unknown and you can count on suffering through the Five Stages, losing more money as you go through each of the stages. As we saw earlier, you can loop back through the first four stages in a vicious circle. You eventually accept the loss, so you might as well set the loss to a predetermined amount and short circuit the Five Stages by going straight to the acceptance stage. Knowing the amount of loss ahead of time reduces the uncertainty factor to nil because you've acknowledged and *accepted* the amount of the potential loss before it occurs.

Not only will the plan prevent you from the throes of the Five Stages, but it will also bring the positive attributes of games to the markets (more on this shortly). Market positions are continuous processes that make the future less certain than the either/or outcome of discrete events, such as a hand of cards or a sports event. Remember the horseracing example mentioned earlier where we stopped the race in the middle and let you bet again? Unless you create some *event-defining parameters*, you are in jeopardy of gambling or betting in an environment completely unsuitable for such activities. If you don't have some means of stopping the continuous process, nothing is locked in—profit or loss—and you're leaving yourself open to being pushed and pulled around by fluctuating prices, random news events, and other people's opinions. Every price change or news item can be rationalized by any of the myriad of ways there are to analyze the markets. The analysis becomes its own reward, an end in itself, an attempt to be right, which is simply betting. Therefore, the fluid market environment needs operational parameters that make a discrete event out of a continuous process. A plan does precisely that by creating an ending point for a market position. A plan that determines the stop-loss first enables you to convert a naturally dangerous, continuous process into a finite, discrete event.

Market participants adamantly deny any connection between what they do and gambling games. The argument is: "There is only the slightest analogy between playing games for money and the conduct of business in a market economy. The characteristic feature of a game is the antagonism of two or more players or teams, whereas the markets are for supplying the wants of consumers."[15] They don't want other people to think they are gamblers so they spend a lot of time explaining how and why the markets aren't the same as casinos. But remember from chapter 7 that most people don't know which type of risk activity they are participating in. They also don't understand that it is the characteristics displayed, not the activity itself, that define whether they are betting, gambling, speculating, trading, or investing. This lack of understanding means people are prone to exhibit the traits of betting or gambling on a continuous process (i.e., the market) rather than a discrete event where such activities belong. Apparently, many market participants reject the casino view of the market in word but not in deed.

However, from my trading and gambling experiences I have learned that the more the markets are treated as a game, the less likely you are to have losses due to psychological factors. Why? Games have rules and defined ending points. Their participants have a game plan. A plan takes the positive attributes of games (not gambling games per se but the concept of a game) and applies them to the market, giving you the structure necessary to create a discrete event. This means you won't confuse Speculating with betting or gambling. It also prevents you from betting or gambling on a continuous process. Recall that thinking before acting is the definition of Speculation. Mixing up the order of the process (i.e., acting then thinking), is betting or gambling. Trying to be *right* (i.e., betting) about an event that never ends means that you will never be completely right. Trying to get excitement (i.e., gambling) from an event that never ends will provide you with more excitement than you bargained for.

Having a plan requires thinking, which only an individual can do—not a crowd. A crowd cannot think any more than it can eat or drink. There is no such thing as a group brain. Since a plan is about having rules, and since mass behavior is not rule governed, having and following a plan means, by definition, you are not part of the crowd. Following your plan imposes discipline over your emotions. Since discipline means not doing what your emotions would have you do, then if you don't have the discipline to follow the plan, your emotions have taken control and you wind up in the crowd. If you don't have control of your emotions via a plan, then your decision making will be based on emotions. That makes you highly subject to contagion because of the hypnotic effect of the changing prices, and you fall into either one of the psychological crowd models mentioned earlier since the crowd epitomizes emotionalism. So rather than monitoring yourself for evidence of each individual emotion, if you avoid the characteristics of crowd behavior you will, by default, avoid emotional decision making. As my mom used to say, "Weak is he who allows his actions to be controlled by his emotions, and strong is he who forces his actions to control his emotions." If you're not consciously doing the latter, then you're unconsciously doing the former, which is precisely Le Bon's description of the conscious personality of an individual vanishing when he enters the crowd.

This last section has been a detailed explanation of how following a plan keeps you from falling into the three-part psychological trap discussed in chapters 6, 7, and 8. Obviously, the three don't have to occur in the order we covered them. That was simply the order given in the definition of psychology back in chapter 5. The errors can occur in any sequence and form a vicious circle. For example, you could (1) make a crowd trade after falling into one of the crowd models previously outlined, then (2) confuse the different types of risk activities and wind up betting because you're only interested in being right, and, finally, (3) personalize a loss when it develops and go through the Five Stages of Internal Loss. Or you could easily reverse the order of numbers two and three or the whole sequence, for that matter. The permutations are there for you to work out, but the point to understand is that these three mistakes feed on one another and lead to one another regardless of which one you fall into first.

Figure 9.1 is a flow chart that gives you the visual representation of what happens when you do not have and follow a plan.

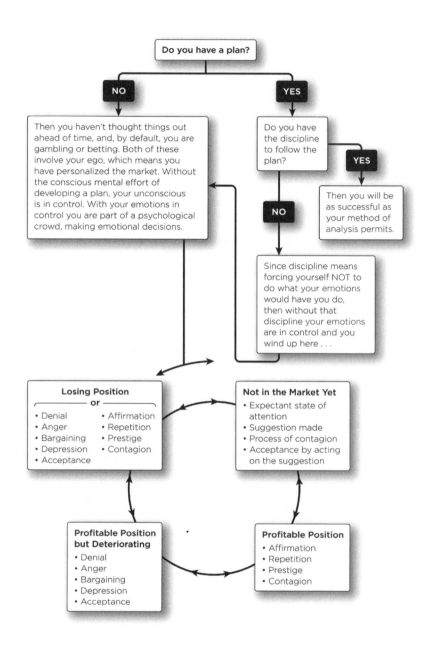

A PLAN AND OBJECTIVITY

The failure to have and follow a plan is the root cause of most of the other "reasons" (or, more accurately, "excuses") for losing money in the markets. And while you will still lose *some* money with a plan, you are certain to lose all your money, eventually, without one. You will enter the market and *then* draw up your possible courses of action on an as-needed basis. Unless your timing is perfect, which may happen occasionally but probably not often, immediately after establishing a market position it is either going to show a profit then a loss, or a loss then a profit. But it will be a loss at some point and you will say, "If only I had sold instead of bought, I would have a profit now instead of a loss." After a series of such trades, you would say, "All those losses would have been profits and I'd be up x amount dollars." Nonsense! Since your timing will in all likelihood never be perfect, the market would have been against you at some point, providing you plenty of opportunity to make an emotional decision and lose money. You must have a means to remove yourself from "subjectively experiencing" the market while making decisions. Obversely stated, you must have a means to "objectively perceive" the market while making decisions and to maintain that *objectivity* once you're in the market. That's exactly what a plan does.

For the roulette player, the last moment of objectivity is just before he places his bet and the wheel starts spinning, after which he can't do anything to lose more money than he wagered. For the market participant, the last moment of objectivity is the moment before he enters the market, after which he *can* still do plenty to lose more money. This is why you must determine your exit and entry criteria during the pretrade, objective time period when your thinking is clear. You wouldn't sign off on an unacceptable loss before entering the market, so the decision about how much you're willing to lose must be made before you get in the market. This keeps you from making or remaking decisions after you have established a position when you would be prone to personalize the market and succumb to the errors discussed in chapters 6, 7, and 8.

All effective decision making requires maintaining one's objectivity through the use of a plan, regardless of the type of decision being made. To drive this point home, consider the following example. A PBS program on human organ transplantation reported, "The reasons people say no to organ donation vary—few people have actually *thought* about their deaths and don't *plan* for it. Family members often haven't discussed their wishes about organ donation *ahead of time. At a time of crisis the decision can be too traumatic.*"[16] They don't have any objectivity. They are looking at a loved one lying on a table, body still warm, heart monitor going, but brain dead. Facing a personal and subjective loss, they quickly succumb to the Five Stages of Internal Loss. This same phenomenon afflicts investors and traders who haven't planned ahead of time. Under pressure in the time of crisis, emotions determine their decisions and actions. On the other hand, a plan establishes objective criteria and forces you to distinguish between decision making based on thinking and decision making based on emotions (i.e., emotionalism). What's the difference? Thought-based decisions are deductive while emotion-based are inductive. Inductive puts acting before thinking, establishing a market position and then doing the work, selectively emphasizing the supporting evidence and ignoring the nonsupporting evidence. Deductive thinking, on the other hand, is consistent with the "thinking before acting" sequence of a plan: doing all of your homework/analysis and then, by default, arriving at a conclusion of whether, what, and when to buy and sell.

Another way of looking at it is: are you long because you're bullish or bullish because you're long? If you're bullish because you're long, your decision was inductive and you will look for reasons, other people's opinions, or anything to keep you in your position—anything to keep you from looking stupid or admitting you are *wrong*. Invariably, you find what you are looking for to justify staying in a losing position, and the losses will mount. In his book *Teaching Thinking*, internationally renowned education expert Edward de Bono says, "A person will use his thinking to keep himself right. This is especially true with more able pupils whose ego has been built up over the years on the basis that they are brighter than other pupils. Thinking is no longer used as an exploration of the subject area but as an ego support device."[17] That sounds exactly like me. My ego had been built up over the years because events seemed to indicate I was a little better than other people. Using thinking in this manner is similar to the inductive decision making mentioned above: it *starts* with a conclusion and *then* looks for evidence to support it. De Bono's comments describe how people use their thinking when they personalize their market positions. When people personalize a string of *successes* (or profits) and an unfolding failure (or loss) develops, having come to believe they are infallible, they use all their intelligence as an ego-support device to prove that they are right, rather than as a means to determine an appropriate course of action. When people personalize *losses*, they use their thinking to protect *themselves*, thereby rationalizing holding onto the position and distorting facts to support their view that they are "right," not "wrong."

Philosopher-novelist Ayn Rand was asked one time in a radio interview whether she thought gun-control laws violated the Second Amendment right to bear arms. "I don't know," she responded, "I haven't thought about it." And she said it in a manner as though it was the most natural thing in the world *not* to have an answer or opinion. Now here is one of the towering geniuses of the twentieth century and the architect of an entire philosophical system saying, "I don't know." Contrast her approach to that of most people who have prepackaged intellectual positions, views, opinions, and answers on almost every topic, gathered from television, newspapers, newsletters, and conversations. Similar to inserting a cassette into a cassette player, they insert the packaged opinions into their minds and hit the playback button whenever they are asked a question. Some people don't even wait to be asked; they offer their regurgitated two cents' worth on every topic they happen upon in conversation. This is particularly true for people's opinions about the markets. That prepackaging is the essence of being in the crowd because, as LeBon points out, crowds always stand in need of ready-made opinions on all subjects. Therefore, having to have an opinion on everything or answer for everything puts you into a crowd mentality. As soon as you express an opinion you have personalized the market, concerned yourself with being right, and entered the crowd. Contrast this to Rand's approach: refrain from answering until you can think about the subject. Following this approach keeps you objective (Rand's philosophy is called objectivism, coincidentally enough), and your thinking can be used to explore the possibilities for an appropriate answer rather than supporting your ego after expressing an opinion.

Remember, participating in the markets is not about egos and being right or wrong (i.e., opinions and betting), and it's not about entertainment (i.e., excitement and gambling). Participating in the markets is about making money; it's about decision making implemented by a plan. And if implemented properly, it's actually quite boring waiting for your buy/sell criteria to materialize. The minute it starts getting exciting, you are gambling.

The only way to combat falling into the *opinion trap* is to follow Rand's lead: think before you answer—if you even answer. If someone asks you what you think about the market, avoid personalizing the market by answering something along the lines of: "According to the method of analysis I use and the rules I use to implement the analysis, if the market does thus and such, I'll do this. If the market does such and thus, I'll do the other." This response expresses your deductive thinking in the form of an objective plan rather than inductive thinking in the form of a subjective opinion. The response is also consistent with viewing the market objectively instead of subjectively, which would lead to personalizing your successes and profits as well as your failures and losses. Answering in the manner just described is not an attempt to absolve you of responsibility for your decisions. On the contrary, taking responsibility and taking something personally are two different things. It is possible to accept responsibility for the ultimate outcome of a decision without internalizing the intervening upswings and downdrafts and postponing the final outcome to the constantly postponed future, hoping the loss will turn around so you can be *right*.

It was pointed out earlier that confused semantics is responsible for a lot of the confused thinking about the market. Your choice of words has a powerful effect on how you regard the market and reveals which of the five types of participant you are. For example, if you say, "I'm right," or "I'm not wrong," you are a bettor and you have implicated your ego, which invariably you will try to protect. If the home team loses a game you *could* say "we lost," and thereby implicate your ego in the losing event. You could even claim, "We didn't lose," and make excuses like: "The officials made bad calls," or, "A good player was sidelined with an injury." That's internalizing an external loss. But how much harm is done? If you bet fifty dollars on the game, you can make excuses and maintain the perspective that you actually won. And doing so won't cost you an extra cent because you still only lost the fifty dollars. But if you don't predetermine how much you can lose and are willing to lose in the market, the "I'm not wrong" or "I'm not losing" perspective will wipe you out.

The lesson here is: Taking either success or failure personally means, by definition, that your ego has become involved and you are in jeopardy of incurring losses due to psychological factors. And we have already discussed that these are the type of losses that are so devastating. They cause the small loss to become a bigger loss and then become a disaster. Remember, Edison didn't take the failures or losses personally, and he succeeded brilliantly (no pun intended). If, *unlike* Edison, you take the failures personally or, like Henry Ford, you take the successes personally, you are setting yourself up for disaster. If your estimate of your self-worth rises and falls with your successes and failures, wins and losses, profitable and unprofitable business transactions, then your self-concept will be in a constant state of crisis. Having tied your self-worth to the vicissitudes of factors beyond your control, you will be primarily concerned with protecting your ego rather than trying to determine an appropriate course of action.

A person's self image "should not be dependent on *particular* successes or failures, since these are not necessarily in a man's direct, volitional control and/or not in his exclusive control. If a person judges himself by criterion that entail factors outside his volitional control, the result, unavoidably, is a precarious self-esteem that is in chronic jeopardy."[18] Therefore, your self-image should not be a function of *what* you have accomplished but *how* you have gone about doing it. Think of it this way: if you have a million dollars in the bank but you stole it, your self-esteem can't be very high. If you earned it, your self-esteem is quite high. Therefore, judge yourself by the degree to which you objectively defined the parameters/conditions that would constitute an opportunity and how well you adhered to them. In other words, pat yourself on the back or kick yourself in the backside depending on whether you develop a plan from a method of analysis, implement the plan via rules, and then follow the rules.

As we saw earlier, people lose in the markets not because of the particular type of method of analysis they use but because of the psychological factors involved in how they fail to apply their particular method. The only way to control those losses is with a preestablished plan. Participating in the markets without a plan is like ordering from a menu that has no prices and then letting the waiter fill out and sign your charge card receipt. It's like playing roulette without knowing in advance how much you had bet and only after the wheel stopped letting the croupier tell you how much you lost or won. If you wouldn't do that in a restaurant or in a casino, why would you do it in the market that has so many more variables and so much more money involved? Operating without a plan, given the fact that a market position can continue indefinitely, makes the future even more uncertain, and you are apt to lose a lot of money if you haven't preplanned your actions. Without a plan your losses grow while you're being pushed and pulled around by price movements, random news events, and what other people say. Therefore, the disciplined use of a plan, with the stop-loss defined first, is the only way to prevent the losses due to psychological factors. Losses will still occur due to analytical factors, but those losses are normal course-of-business-type losses. If you find those losses intolerable, deal with them by reexamining your method of analysis and refining your rules, but not while you're in the market. The point is to keep from compounding those losses with losses due to psychological factors.

All effective plans require eliminating the losses due to psychology by defining a stop-loss first, even plans and decision making that don't involve the markets. A recent example came to mind when I was watching the news one night in September 1993. Senator Sam Nunn commented on the idea of sending U.S. troops to Bosnia: "We ought to have an exit strategy before committing troops."[19] Senator Bob Dole echoed Nunn's sentiments in October 1993, when he said "What's it gonna cost? When are you gonna get out?"[20] Before beginning a mission in Bosnia, these senators wanted to know when or under what set of circumstances the mission would end.

In the same way in which Shell applied scenario planning to a wide variety of situations in very different realms, applying our parable to all decision making is not as far-fetched as it first may seem. To make the point, consider a slightly less recent public-policy example: Lyndon Johnson and the Vietnam War. LBJ did essentially the same thing I did, starting with his belief in past successes. When LBJ considered committing ground forces to Vietnam, he "did so with blind faith buttressed by remembered victories: The United States always won."[21] As Johnson began to escalate the war in early 1965, protests erupted from students, teachers, senators, and columnists. Then in April, in response to a series of coups in the Dominican Republic, Johnson sent 22,000 troops to the Caribbean island. He also sent Secretary of State McGeorge Bundy to negotiate a settlement. The protesters became even louder about this U.S. intervention. But a noncommunist government was elected, and the U.S. forces withdrew. This made the critics of the Johnson's foreign policy look and sound like they didn't know what they were talking about. His success in the Dominican Republic fed his ego, gave him a sense of the Midas touch syndrome, and reinforced his conviction that *he* was right, and anyone who disagreed with him was wrong.

As the war progressed, the United States became more heavily involved. LBJ would come to micromanage the situation in Vietnam, picking some bombing sites himself and approving most others. He would rise at two a.m. (to adjust for the time change) and go to the war room in the basement of the White House so he could monitor developments in Vietnam. Johnson began to identify his personal worth with success in Vietnam. As evidence, consider "LBJ's impression that he couldn't *lose* Vietnam and keep allies or win elections."[22] Johnson had personalized and internalized Vietnam because, for him, it meant his reputation.

It's not as though LBJ wasn't encouraged to consider an exit strategy—a stop-loss in Vietnam, so to speak. McGeorge Bundy sent Johnson a memo suggesting "hard analysis on such questions as . . . What is the upper limit of our liability?" if the United States committed ground troops.[23] In essence, Bundy wanted to know what the U.S. stop-loss was going to be. In October 1964, Under-Secretary of State George Ball wrote an internal memo that argued that South Vietnam was a lost cause. Ball was acknowledging a loss as a loss. Unfortunately, "to question the ability of the United States to succeed militarily was to challenge Johnson's pride."[24]

This isn't to say Johnson should have listened to every Tom, Dick, and Harry advisor. It simply shows you another example of how all decision makers can fall prey to the same errors I did. LBJ did not have an exit strategy, much less an entire plan formed after objective decision making. In fact, according to one of his aides, "it was Johnson's custom to reach a decision inwardly and *then* make it appear the decision was the result of consultation and debate."[25] That was inductive decision making. Instead of starting with a blank slate, analyzing the situation, and arriving at a decision deductively, he inductively took a position and then searched for evidence to support that original position. Put all this together and you have a classic case of someone who personalized previous successes and assumed he would succeed *simply because* he was involved in the current undertaking. Having personalized the situation, he saw loss as the same thing as *wrong*, which his ego couldn't take. Therefore, all subsequent decisions revolved around protecting *him*. His thinking became, as de Bono put it, an ego-support device instead of a means of objective decision making. With no formalized plan beginning with an exit strategy, he became a victim of the same process I did when I was in the bean-oil position. He internalized the developing loss in Vietnam, confused *being right* with *doing right* (i.e., doing the most prudent thing), and succumbed to emotional decision making. What might LBJ have done instead? Two professors from Harvard say LBJ should have assessed the downside exposure and created a plan to handle it:

> The President might also have paused longer over the question Bundy had posed . . . about "the limit of our liability." Johnson might have begun to ponder in 1965 the speech he ought to give in 1966 if certain conditions were not fulfilled by then—and what those conditions might be. He might, in short, have planned a test for his presumptions . . . as all decision-makers should routinely do.[26]

Commit the Plan to Paper

After you have developed your plan, start preparing your speech, so to speak, about what you're going to do if certain conditions aren't fulfilled by a certain time and what those conditions are. Like any good speech writer, you should start by putting pen to paper. To prevent unintentional and implicit violation of your plan, no device is more effective than setting down that plan before your eyes explicitly in black and white. This objectifies, externalizes, and depersonalizes your thinking, so you can hold yourself accountable.

To take an example from business, look at powerhouse securities firm Morgan Stanley, one of the most profitable financial institutions in the country. Ever since it converted from a private partnership to a publicly traded company in 1986, Morgan Stanley has achieved the highest average return on equity of any publicly traded U.S. securities firm.[27] It's "avoided disasters and seized opportunities" because it is "fanatical about planning for any contingency, good or bad."[28] And the firm carries out that planning by having staffers *write* detailed reports about all the consequences for the firm if certain hypothetical events came to pass. The worst-case scenarios are compiled in what the firm calls blue books. "'We're constantly writing these stupid blue books,' grumbles one Morgan Stanley principal. 'It definitely slows us down.' On the other hand, he concedes with a shrug, 'We don't make any mistakes.'"[29] Whether Morgan Stanley makes mistakes is open to debate, but its mistakes are contained. Its commitment to planning, as well as committing those plans to writing, has kept the firm out of disastrous situations.

CONCLUSION

It's not wise to violate the rules until you know how to observe them.

—T. S. ELIOT

In 1965 Steve McQueen starred in The Cincinnati Kid, *the classic poker movie of all time. In the climactic scene of the movie, Steve McQueen (The Kid) and Edward G. Robinson (The Man) play a final hand of five-card stud. The Kid is trying to dethrone The Man in a winner-take-all five-card-stud poker game that has lasted several days and eliminated all of the other players.*

With three cards dealt, McQueen's two up cards are a pair of tens, and he bets heavily, $1,000. Robinson is showing the queen and the eight of diamonds. That is a lousy hand for Robinson, but he calls the bet and raises $1,000. He is betting as though his hole card is a queen or he somehow thinks he will get a straight flush. Or he is pulling the bluff of the century. Robinson's next card is the ten of diamonds and McQueen's is the ace of clubs. McQueen bets $3,000. A smart move. Robinson calls and raises. Robinson is playing for the straight flush, not a pair of queens. Or he is bluffing. Robinson's fifth card is the nine of diamonds, and McQueen gets the ace of spades. McQueen bets all he has in front of him, $3,500. "That ace must have helped you, Kid. I'll call your thirty-five-hundred and raise you five-thousand," says Robinson.

Now, if you can't call a bet, you fold and go home unless the other player is willing to take your marker (an IOU). Well, McQueen is out of money, and the only way he can continue is if Robinson will take McQueen's *marker. In order to stay in the game, McQueen agrees to give Robinson an IOU for $5,000. The only card that can beat McQueen is the jack of diamonds. McQueen asks to see Robinson's hole card. Robinson turns over the jack of diamonds. McQueen looks as though he's going to throw up. He has been wiped out. McQueen's full house, aces over tens, loses to Robinson's straight flush.*

The dealer is incredulous. "You're raising tens on a lousy three flush?" she says to Robinson. She was right! Robinson never should have made that bet since he had only the slim makings of a straight flush and he was staring at McQueen's pair of tens. You don't often beat two pair, and certainly not a full house.

"Gets down to what it's all about doesn't it? Making the wrong move at the right time. Like life I guess . . ." says Robinson to the dealer.

A poker player risks his money not knowing the cards he will draw or what cards the other players will draw. When you wager in poker, you either try to tell the other players what you've got in your hand (a lockjaw player) or you try not to tell them what you've got (a loose player) or you try to get them to think you've got something you don't have (also a loose player), all depending on what your agenda is. The good poker player tries to alternate between being a lockjaw player and a loose player. In other words, measured inconsistency is the key to winning in poker. A lockjaw player is someone who never stays in the game unless he's got a hand. He folds almost every hand. He antes and he's gone, antes and he's gone. The message is that if he's in, everybody else is playing for second place because the only time he's in is when he has a good hand. If everybody at the table believes the only time he's in the game is when he has a good hand, occasionally he can bluff and get away with it.

For example: I'm playing five-card stud, and my first up card is a jack, my down card is a three and somebody else has a king showing. He bets $5 and I call his $5 and raise $10. If everybody at the table thinks that I stay in the game only when I've got something, that I'm lockjaw, then everybody thinks I have two jacks. Now everybody is playing against the two jacks even if I don't have two jacks. If you get the reputation of lockjaw, you have set up the opportunity to fake—to bluff. You can only get to that point if you have folded a lot of hands and if when you have stayed in, you won or finished a very close second. To build that reputation you've got to fold much more that you stay, and when you stay you've got to win. Once you get that reputation and live by it, not only do you save a lot of money by folding early when you have a bad hand, but you have the opportunity to bluff occasionally. More frequent bluffers are also loose poker players. They try to mislead the other players by betting heavily on a poor hand or betting lightly on a good one. The more you are caught bluffing, the more likely you will be able to really take someone to the cleaners when you have a good hand.

Like the poker player, the investor risks his money not knowing how the individual company, stocks in general, or the economy as a whole will perform. While measured inconsistency may be the key to success in poker, disciplined consistency is the key to success in the markets once you've developed rules and made it a game. Having and following a plan doesn't guarantee success, nor does it make you infallible. However, a plan is necessary for consistent loss control. There is nothing to learn from the bluffing aspect of poker, but there is something to learn from part of the lockjaw poker player's strategy. Which part? The part he uses to build his reputation: he stays when he has a hand and gets out when he doesn't have a hand. Your plan is structured so that you stay when your position is working and you get out when it's not. Take the loss, and don't worry about it. Sticking to the discipline of your plan enables you to stay when you have a good situation and forces you to forfeit the ante when you don't. If you drop your discipline and try bluffing, you're exposing yourself to losing all of your money.

To bluff means to intimidate by showing more confidence than the facts support. If you try to bluff the market by breaking your rules, you will eventually lose your money. Oh sure, you might break the rules a couple of times and get away with it. You might even get away with it several times. But if you try to bluff the market by staying in a losing trade and it comes back and turns into a profit, what have you learned? You have learned that doing the wrong thing pays off, which means you will try to bluff again. The problem is: you won't be able to distinguish between the times when it's safe to break the rules and when it's not.

So, yes, there are times when breaking your rules still results in a profit. You can be rewarded for doing the "wrong thing," and you can be rewarded for doing the "right thing" for the wrong reason. I did that a lot during the early part of my life. However, if you continue to do the wrong thing in the market and get rewarded, your profits won't be linked to any particular recurring set of circumstances or rule following on your part. This will result in what psychologists call a random reward schedule, the strongest form of reinforcement for getting a person to repeat a behavior. For example, consider the psychologist who wants a monkey to repeat the behavior of pressing a button. The experiment involves having food released into the cage when the monkey presses the button a certain number of times. The psychologist might set the mechanism to release the food after it has been hit a fixed number of times, for example, every five times, or he might set it to release the food after a variable number of times, for example, five times, then seven, then three, then twelve. The monkey will hit the button more if the reward interval is varied than if it is fixed. When the reward interval is varied, the monkey will simply keep hitting the button until the reward appears, believing it is inevitable.

One of the best trades I ever made was an $8,000 loss on a short gold trade; I got stopped out at $350 per ounce on its way to $875. One day in early August 1979, the gold market shot above $300 for the first time ever. I thought that was a ridiculous price and sold short two gold contracts at $310. Then I gave an order to a friend of mine to stop me out at $317, left the floor, and went to my accountant's office to finish my 1978 taxes before the August 15 extended deadline ran out. Later that day, while I was meeting with my accountant, I got a call from my secretary. The Board of Governors of the Chicago Mercantile Exchange (of which I was a member) had called an emergency meeting. The gold market had closed in the United States for the day, but it was trading fifty dollars higher in Hong Kong, and we had to vote on whether to change the daily permissible limit on the gold futures contract at the CME from ten dollars to thirty dollars. (Needless to say, I recused myself from the vote).

I did exactly the "right thing," so to speak, of planning the trade, putting in the stop, entering the market, and then leaving the stop alone. But the only reason I left the stop alone is because I had given the order to someone else and I was too embarrassed to go to him to cancel it. In effect, I did "the right" thing for "the wrong" reason. At the time, I didn't learn the proper lesson from that experience. I hated the idea of leaving the stop in, but I knew I had to because I didn't want the embarrassment of going to my friend and saying, in effect, "I'm so stupid that I want to cancel my stop and stay short this market." All I got out of that experience was that it was more important to me not to feel embarrassed than it was to make money. I was like the monkey in the psychologist's cage, repeating behaviors that sometimes produced profits and sometimes losses but not knowing which was which.

Doing the "wrong thing" (i.e., breaking your rules) in the markets and still being rewarded means you will repeat behavior that may or may not have been responsible for the profitable trade or investment. If you don't know what is making the profitable trades profitable, you won't know what to repeat in order to repeat the profits (or avoid losses). Your profits won't be linked to any specific behavior on your part. This means you're only going to be allowed to make a bad decision once—and you know you will do it at least once. You don't know if it will be this time, next time, or the time after that. But you will do it. And if you bluff, you *will* lose your money. If you deviate from your plan you are playing with a lighted fuse. Sure, the bomb may not go off in any particular battle, but before the war is over, the bomb will explode in your face.

WHAT IF . . . ?

Robinson's comment about "making the wrong move at the right time" is another way of saying "deviating from the plan and basing your decision on a hunch, feeling, or intuition." It's like taking a multiple-choice test in school, not knowing the answer, and going with your gut. It's like the time Conrad doubled his bet at the baccarat table because he got a *feeling* that we were going to get a run.

The market is no place for "making the wrong move at the right time." Any deviation from your plan triggers the potential for losses due to psychological factors. It cannot be emphasized enough how important it is for you to stick to your plan. If you get nothing else from this book except the acknowledgment that you need a plan, then at least you'll know when you're deviating. At least you will know that you are deviating from *something* whereas prior to reading the book you would not have known. However, you also cannot ignore the fact that even after reading this book, at some point in the future you will deviate from your plan and break the rules.

Even though the following advice may seem to contradict everything this book has said about the need for a plan, I would be remiss if I didn't give you this final lesson about the markets because I know you're human, and I know you will deviate. If you deviate from your plan, break the rules, follow a tip, act on some intuition or gut feel, remember this: Speculating (and this includes investing and trading) is the only human endeavor in which what feels good is the right thing to do. We all know we shouldn't smoke; a lot of us still do. We know we shouldn't drink; a lot of us still do. We know we shouldn't drive over the speed limit; a lot of us do. Why do we do all these things that are not good for us and that we know are not good for us? Well, because they feel good. It feels good to drink and smoke and drive fast. But ever since we were little kids we have been told not to do things that feel good. When it comes to the markets you're supposed to do what feels good. If you deviate from your plan and the market starts going against you, what are you going to say when I knock on your door and ask, "Well? Are you having fun? Is this an enjoyable experience?" You're going to say, "No! This is not fun. Looking at these prices going down is not fun." You know what you should do? Don't go looking for supporting evidence or reasons to stay in the market. Do what feels good. Get out. There is an inverse relationship between your threshold of pain and success in the markets, so as soon as you feel the pain: get out. What if you have on a long position and prices are going up, does that feel good? Do you know what you're supposed to do? Keep feeling good; leave it alone. It's working fine. Stay with positions that make you feel good; get out of positions that make you feel bad. You'll know when you feel bad; if you can recognize anything, you will recognize "this doesn't feel good." The minute it doesn't feel good, stop doing it. It's that simple.

POSTSCRIPT

In the preface, we saw that Henry Ford personalized his successes and lost nearly a billion dollars by following his opinions to the bitter end. But Henry Ford wasn't the only businessperson who personalized his successes and then suffered a huge loss.

Sir Freddie Laker, the British entrepreneur, started a no-frills transatlantic airline service, Skytrain, in 1977. Laker's story is the classic one of a factory tea boy who, through hard work and effort, turned himself into a jet-setting millionaire. In order to achieve fortune and fame, he had taken on both the U.S. and British governments and the International Air Transport Association, the international airline cartel. Granted, the service was only across the North Atlantic, but it would spread to all routes—wouldn't it? All this warrior had to do was to take on those representatives of the establishment a few more times.

A combination of factors, including adverse currency movements and the U.S. government grounding of all DC10 airplanes in 1979 right at the start of the peak holiday traffic season, began to strain Laker's financial situation. As the storm clouds gathered around Laker Airways, Laker dismissed the idea that he was under severe financial strain: "No, I am not bust!" (Sound like denial to you?) He maintained this position even after it became obvious that the airline would not be able to meet the $48 million repayment of interest and principal needed between September 1981 and March 1982. Offensively, Laker told the bankers that he was going to teach them their jobs. "I have innovated in aviation; now I must innovate in banking," he boasted. (Sound like emotionalism, i.e., the prestige in a crowd decision?) Right up until the last minute, Sir Freddie Laker maintained that all was going to turn out satisfactorily; his airline was not going to go broke. But it wasn't to be. On Thursday, February 4, 1982, at eight a.m., the receivers were called in.[1]

Also consider the case of personal-computer pioneer and whiz kid Steve Jobs. With no formal training in computing, Jobs divined the shape of things to come. His once unconventional ideas, which foresaw the personal-computer revolution, proved prescient. After creating Apple II, the first wildly successful and popular personal computer, Jobs led and inspired the team that created the most acclaimed PC, the Macintosh. His "faith in his own genius," as the *Wall Street Journal* called it, which served him well at Apple, helped precipitate his fall from a very lofty perch when he started his subsequent computer company, NeXT. He ignored advisors' repeated warnings about flaws in NeXT's strategy and stuck tenaciously to his vision. This time, however, Jobs's vision proved flawed. NeXT has never turned a net profit and has exhausted $250 million from backers.[2]

As a final example, look at the story of Roy Raymond, who started the highly successful chain of seductive and elegant lingerie stores, Victoria's Secret. In 1982, he sold the business to The Limited for $2 million. Says a friend of Mr. Raymond's, "Roy had that feeling that he was bulletproof and that whatever he touched would turn to gold."[3] His next endeavor was an upscale children's clothing store which plunged him into bankruptcy proceedings.

Each of these men personalized his successes and began to believe he would only ever have success. On the other hand, consider Roberto Goizueta, CEO of Coca-Cola. When Goizueta became president in 1981, he created a "Strategy for the 1980s," which spelled out his intention to "diversify Coca-Cola into services that complement our product lines and that are compatible with our consumer image."[4]

Few people, including the media, took him seriously. Then in 1983 Coke purchased Columbia Pictures. People were aghast. "Financial analysts dumped on the deal claiming Coke had paid too much, and besides—what did Coke know about making movies?"[5] Coke's stock dropped 10 percent within a few days. During the rest of that year, however, critics had to admit that Coke (and Goizueta) hadn't been so dumb after all. Columbia cranked out three smash hits in a row: *Tootsie*, *Ghandi*, and *The Toy*. Goizueta also introduced the idea of lending the magical Coke name to another soft drink, an idea most people at the Company viewed as heretical. In fact, when a few daring men suggested the same idea in the early 1960s while developing Tab, then-CEO J. Paul Austin condemned them for it. Two decades later here was Austin's replacement proposing to lend the Coke name to a diet soft drink. Diet Coke was an instant phenomenon, surpassing all company expectations.

"By the end of 1983, Goizueta felt vindicated in the eyes of the world. Columbia, a money machine, earned $91 million in its first full year as a Coca-Cola subsidiary. In 1983, following hard on the heels of diet Coke's unparalleled achievement, the company introduced caffeine-free versions of Coca-Cola, diet Coke and TaB. Goizueta proved that Coke could adapt, and once the giant stirred, it usually dominated a market segment."[6] Goizueta's triumph intensified, dominating a 1983 spring issue of *Business Week*, being named by *Ad-Week* "marketer of the year" and being praised by *Dun's Business Month* for running one of America's five best-managed companies.[7] It would seem that Roberto Goizueta had every reason for self-congratulation. Yet in 1983 he said, "There is a danger when a company is doing as well as we are. And that is, to think that we can do no wrong: we can do wrong and we can do wrong big."[8]

In 1985, Goizueta decided to change Coke's secret formula. He had been a chemist at Coke for many years, and the idea of changing the formula had been around for a long time. He announced the change to New Coke at a press conference on April 19, 1985. Goizueta called it the "boldest single marketing move in the history of the packaged consumer goods business," and also the "surest move ever made."[9] There was immediate disapproval from the media and public. *Business Week* called the decision the marketing blunder of the decade and many others agreed. But "the ready, fire! aim philosophy had worked so far, and this audacious, bold move would prove Coca-Cola's leadership to any doubters."[10]

Is it possible Goizueta had personalized his previous successes? Was he experiencing the Midas touch syndrome? He had made several major decisions with which others disagreed, yet each time he had been proven right. Unlike Ford, Laker, Jobs, and Raymond, Goizueta didn't personalize his previous successes, so he was able to recognize and accept the "loss." He didn't make the matter an issue of personal pride and choose to fight to the bitter end. He recognized it as a losing proposition to eliminate the original formula altogether. He cut his losses and moved on. He managed the situation brilliantly by reintroducing the original formula under the name Coca-Cola Classic and increased Coca-Cola's market share in the soft drink business in the process.

Why was Goizueta able to avoid entering the trap that produces the fatal errors? Was it because managers are exempt from this pitfall? No. We'll see shortly that managers are quite susceptible. Did Ford, Raymond, and the others succumb because they were entrepreneurs and entrepreneurs have difficulty going on to be managers? No. There are numerous cases of the founding entrepreneur going on to successfully manage the company, for example, Fred Smith at Federal Express, William McGowan at MCI Communications, Bill Gates at Microsoft. So what was it that separated Goizueta the others? They fell into a category aptly described by William Sahlman, professor of business administration, Harvard Business School, this way: "I've seen people who have been at a certain place at a certain point in time with a good idea . . . and did [*sic*] fabulously well, and they haven't a clue about what to do next. They're not good advisors and they're not repeat entrepreneurs. And there's a process of assuming, based on what you've succeeded in doing in the past, that you're a genius."[11] The *process* Sahlman is referring to is the process of personalizing successes as explained in this book. Goizueta avoided the process, and the others didn't. He didn't equate his personal worth with whether or not his idea was successful. He distinguished external successes and losses from internal ones, and he didn't personalize his previous accomplishments. He knew the difference between being right and *doing right*, and he avoided emotionalism. That's what sets the successful decision maker apart from the not-so-successful.

Even though Goizueta was primarily a manager and the others were primarily entrepreneurs, they were all in the business of making decisions, the goal of which is the profits of managing risk, not the ego gratification of being right. Remember, you don't get any money just because you know *why* the market is going up or down. You only get money if your plan has positioned you to capitalize on the market's movement, *regardless* of whether you know why the market is up or down on a particular day.

Harvard Business Review, the bible of management theory, says, "An essential quality needed by a good salesman is a particular kind of ego drive which makes him want to make the sale in a personal or ego way, not merely for the money to be gained. His self-picture improves dramatically by virtue of making the sale and diminishes with failure."[12] It is precisely this quality which is so detrimental to a Speculator and any other type of decision maker. Realizing this helped me understand why I was able to make so much money as a salesman yet couldn't make a dime as a trader. Remember my futile efforts to make all the money back and the realization I had about having never been a trader? I had been a good salesman and at the right place at the right time, not a trader.

This doesn't mean salespeople can't be traders, and it doesn't mean salespeople can't be managers or entrepreneurs. But it does mean that given a salesperson's (i.e., a broker's) motivation, he needs to have a plan that will prevent the market position or his client's position from becoming personalized the way I personalized my clients' losses after I blew up the Cleveland office. The ego drive of a salesperson may also explain why salespeople have a reputation for being lousy traders. How so? A salesperson's goal is to make the sale;

to be right by countering objections and negative feedback from the prospect. But the Speculator's goal is to make money, not to *be right* or counter the negative feedback from the market. A salesman's ego gratification from being right is precisely what the entrepreneur, Speculator, and manager must avoid. Tying one's self-picture to the success or failure of the business venture or market position means the individual will not want to acknowledge a loss when it occurs and will play out the pattern outlined in the flow chart. This is true for all losses resulting from psychological factors, regardless of the scale of the loss in dollar terms ($1,000 or $1,000,000) or the venue in which the loss takes place (in the markets or in other lines of business). For instance, a 1989 study in the *Journal of Accounting Research* concluded that managers are "reluctant to give up on projects they begin because to do so would convey a negative signal about their ability." Moreover, a "manager might not choose to sell the assets because the potential sale would convey negative information about him personally." The study also found that when such a manager was replaced, his "replacement who does not care about the first manager's reputation, would have no such reason for holding onto the assets, and will tend to sell them relatively quickly."[13] The replacement manager was able to be objective; his predecessor wasn't. What does this tell you? Managers and corporate executives can become too attached to a project and personalize it, and they are susceptible to the losses due to psychological factors just like Speculators are when they personalize market positions.

What you have to understand as a Speculator, entrepreneur, or manager is that there is a fine line between perseverance because you think the *idea* is a good one and perseverance because *you* think the idea is a good one. The former is objective. The latter is subjective and often follows personalizing previous successes. In the first case, you arrived at the decision deductively after examining the evidence. The decision is supported by the facts, and you have a pragmatic exit discipline—a defined set of circumstances that will cause you to determine the idea is no longer a good one, because the evidence no longer supports the original decision. In the second case, the decision is made first; with no exit strategy, you inductively seek evidence that will support the decision. In the former, your thinking is used to explore possibilities and you arrive at a conclusion by default; in the latter, your thinking is used to defend a previously expressed opinion and to protect your ego, which is attached to that opinion.

If you didn't understand the distinction about perseverance mentioned above, you might think all you had to do to be a successful entrepreneur was believe in your idea and take on the risk of carrying it out. After all, that's what entrepreneurs do, right? They take risks. Some of them take seemingly huge risks, so huge that entrepreneurs are often compared to daredevils. But are they actually seeking risks?

> Look at Scott Schmidt, the "entrepreneur" who popularized what has become known as extreme skiing. Schmidt jumps from 60-foot cliffs for a living. Ski-equipment companies sponsor him, and people make videos of his jumps. From the chairlift, he appears a reckless maniac. But for every jump, he has carefully charted the takeoff point and landing.... His pioneering work has broken a path for an "industry" of extreme skiers—some of whom have been more reckless and died. Schmidt doesn't consider himself reckless.[14]

Given his approach, Schmidt isn't reckless—he charts (i.e., plans) his entry and exit to the jump. He doesn't seek risk; he seeks to reduce and manage risk.

Look at self-made billionaire entrepreneur Craig McCaw. Despite any appearances to the contrary, Craig McCaw, founder and chairman of McCaw Cellular Communications, maintains that he and those at his company "have always been risk averse."[15] And how did his approach to the business develop? From a game. (Sound familiar?) During early business trips and chess games with J. Elroy McCaw," his father, who was also an entrepreneur, Craig "learned the concept of an *exit strategy*.... Every deal we ever did had a back door. The public just didn't see the back doors."[16] This is just another example of what this book has been saying about the need for a stop-loss (i.e., exit strategy) and of the benefits of applying the positive attributes of a game to the continuous process of business and the markets.

What's true about the markets is also true for business in general. Just as there are many ways to make money in the markets, there are many ways to make money in business. Sam Walton made his money one way, and Gucci made his another way. You can read through the annals of American business and see extraordinary variety in the personalities and methods among the best known entrepreneurs and business people; they come in all shapes and sizes. Some were team efforts, others were individual. Some had a lot of money to get started, others did not. The differences go on and on. There is no single pattern to how the most successful entrepreneurs or the best managers in business make money. However, there is a common denominator among this group: rather than just taking risks, as is commonly assumed, they excel at judging, minimizing, and controlling risks. Craig McCaw understood this; did Steve Jobs? Over a period of eight years, NeXT has "consumed $250 million without producing a successful product or sustained profitability."[17] What is the exit point? The original capital infusion from Ross Perot and Cannon, Inc., was $125 million. Was it known then that the loss might go to $250 million? If so, fine. But if not, what's to keep it from going to $350 million? Managers of all businesses must be able to *take* losses.

Alan "Ace" Greenburg, CEO of Bear Stearns says, "The definition of a trader is a guy who takes losses."[18] This is exactly the point made earlier about losses being a normal part of business and that trying to avoid losses altogether by not taking them is a loser's curse. Bear Stearns has weekly "cold sweat" meetings in which traders are grilled about their positions. The firm tolerates losses but not surprises. In one such meeting, a trader was asked about one of his positions and what the downside was. He outlined several scenarios and the losses associated with each. When the position started to deteriorate, the firm took the mounting losses, upward of $10 million, in stride. They were prepared for such an event. The losses never surpassed their stop-loss point and the position soon turned around and made money. It is important to understand that they held on not because they wanted to look good, look smart, or be right. They held on because the position remained within previously defined and acceptable loss parameters. Remember, people participate in the markets—all markets—either to satisfy a need (i.e., solve a problem) or to satisfy a want (i.e., make them feel good). Managing risk solves a problem and should never be engaged in to feel good, look smart, or *be right.*

In all risk taking—Speculation, business ventures, entrepreneurial activities—it is the loss side on which you must focus first. (This is even true for gambling—the gambler determines how much he's willing to bet, and lose, before the game is played. He doesn't wait for the game to end and then let the croupier or dealer assign his wager for him.) How do you determine the downside, and how do you control or minimize it? With objective decision making and a plan that has as its starting point the stop-loss parameters.

Rather than looking for a formula for success to follow, this book has identified the formula for failure to avoid. As An Wang, founder of Wang Laboratories, said, "It is my belief that there are no 'secrets' to success."[19] The formula for failure is not lack of knowledge, brains, skill, or hard work, and it's not lack of luck; it's personalizing losses, especially if preceded by a string of wins or profits. It's refusing to acknowledge and accept the reality of a loss when it starts to occur because to do so would reflect negatively on you.

APPENDIX

JIM ROGERS formed one half (George Soros was the other half) of the phenomenally successful Soros Fund. During his tenure, 1969–1980, the fund was up 3,365 percent vs. the S&P composite's gain of 47 percent.

MARTY SCHWARTZ is an independent professional trader. He attained a degree of fame from his performance in the U.S. Trading Championships. He entered ten four-month contests and in nine of those contests (in one contest he broke even) he has made more money than all the other contestants combined, averaging 210 percent nonannualized return.

JOHN TEMPLETON is the dean of global investing. His investing record shows that for thirty-one years his performance has averaged an annual increases of 15 percent, versus 7 percent for the Standard & Poor's Index. He managed $6 billion for the Templeton Funds before "retiring."

WILLIAM O'NEIL started in the securities business in 1958 as a stock broker. During 1962–63, he pyramided $5,000 into $200,000 in three back-to-back trades. Eventually he launched the *Investors Business Daily* newspaper. Over the past ten years, his investments have averaged a 40 percent annual return.

WARREN BUFFETT started Buffett Partnership at the age of twenty-five with $100,000. In 1969 when he liquidated the partnership at the speculative market peak, it had grown to $100,000,000. Buffett's take— $25,000,000. His investors earned thirty times their original investment. Today he runs Berkshire Hathaway, and his investors continue to benefit from his stellar performance. His personal investing success is evidenced by his inclusion in the Forbes 400 with a personal net worth of $1 billion.

PETER LYNCH ran Fidelity Management's Magellan Fund, the largest mutual fund in history, from 1977 to 1990. Before retiring in January 1990,

Lynch was one of the highest paid portfolio investment employees in the world. Ten thousand dollars placed with Lynch in 1977 when he took over management of the fund grew to $200,000 in 1988.

PAUL TUDOR JONES earned over a million dollars in commissions in his second year in the business as a commodity broker. In 1980 he switched to the floor of the New York Cotton Exchange and made millions during the next few years. Each $1,000 invested with him as chairman of Tudor Investments in 1984 had grown to more than $17,000 by 1988.

MICHAEL STEINHARDT has one of the best twenty-year track records in investment history. Ten thousand dollars put in his hedge fund at its 1967 inception grew to over $1,000,000 twenty years later, achieving a compounded annual growth rate of 30 percent. Over the same period, $10,000 invested in the Standard & Poor's 500 Index grew to only $64,000.

ROY NEUBERGER is chairman of Neuberger-Berman & Company. He started as a runner on Wall Street in 1929, and when he began investing his own money a few years later, he took $30,000 to several hundred million.

BERNARD BARUCH had made $3,000,000 on Wall Street by the time he was thirty-two years old—and this was in the 1920s and 1930s. He made a million in the stock market, and put it at risk to earn a second million, and so on, until he amassed $25,000,000.

W. D. GANN was one of the most successful commodity and stock traders in the 1920s and 1930s—if not all time. An analysis of his trading record over twenty-five market days revealed that he made 286 trades, 264 of which were profitable. During that period, he turned $450 into $37,000.

NOTES

PART I. REMINISCENCES OF A TRADER

1. "The Five Deadly Business Sins," *Wall Street Journal*, October 21, 1993.

2. An Wang, *Lessons: An Autobiography* (Reading, Mass.: Addison Wesley, 1986), p. 1.

3. Herb Kelleher, television advertisement for American Express, Olgivy & Mather, 1993.

5. THE QUEST

1. Jack Schwager, *Market Wizards: Interviews with Top Traders* (New York: New York Institute of Finance, 1989), p. 317.

2. Ibid., p. 265.

3. Madelon DeVoe Talley, *The Passionate Investors* (New York: Crown, 1987), pp. 70–72.

4. Schwager, *Market Wizards*, p. 229.

5. Talley, *The Passionate Investors*, pp. 75–78.

6. Ibid., p. 110.

7. Schwager, *Market Wizards*, p. 232.

8. Talley, *The Passionate Investors*, p. 110.

9. Ibid., p. 29.

10. Schwager, *Market Wizards*, pp. 314–15.

11. Ibid., p. 129.

12. Talley, *The Passionate Investors*, p. 52.

13. Schwager, *Market Wizards*, p. 291.

14. Ibid., p. 197.

15. W. D. Gann, *How to Make Profits in Commodities* (Pomeroy, Wash.: Lambert-Gann, 1951), p. 18.

16. John Train, *The New Money Masters* (New York: Harper and Row, 1989), p. 22.

17. Schwager, *Market Wizards*, pp. 276, 279.

18. Ibid.,,, pp. 126, 136.

19. "Where's the Buffet? I Missed Warren at His Favorite Steakhouse," *Money* (August 1991): p. 72.

20. Schwager, *Market Wizards*, p. 233

21. Talley, *The Passionate Investors*, p. 29.

7. THE PSYCHOLOGICAL FALLACIES OF RISK

1. Edward O. Thorp, *Beat the Dealer: A Winning Strategy for the Game of Twenty-one* (New York: Vintage, 1966), p. 182.

2. Peter Drucker, *Management* (New York: Harper Row, 1985), p. 512.

3. "Confessions of a Compulsive High-Roller," *Business Week*, July 29, 1991, p. 78.

4. Richard A. Epstein, *The Theory of Gambling and Statistical Logic* (New York: Academic Press, 1977), pp. 393–94.

5. Ludwig von Mises, *Human Action: A Treatise on Economics* (Chicago: Contemporary, 1966), p. 116.

8. THE PSYCHOLOGICAL CROWD

1. Gustave Le Bon, *The Crowd: A Study of the Popular Mind* (New York: The Macmillan Co., 1896).

2. Charles P. Kindleberger, *Manias, Panics, and Crashes: A History of Financial Crises* (New York: Basic, 1989), pp. 17–18.

3. Le Bon, *The Crowd*, pp. 2–3.

4. Humphrey Neil, *The Art of Contrary Thinking* (Caldwell, Idaho: Caxton Printers, 1954), p. 137.

5. Ibid., pp. 8–10.

6. Irving L. Janus, *Victims of Groupthink: A Psychological Study of Foreign-Policy Decisions and Fiascoes* (Boston: Houghton Mifflin, 1972), p. 87.

7. Neil, *The Art of Contrary Thinking*, p. 134.

9. RULES, TOOLS, AND FOOLS

1. James Grant, testimony before the House Banking Committee, July 30, 1992.

2. Henry Hazlitt, *The Failure of the "New Economics": An Analysis of the Keynesian Fallacies* (Lanham, Md.: University Press of America, 1983), p. 183.

3. Ludwig von Mises, *Human Action: A Treatise on Economics* (Chicago: Contemporary, 1966), pp. 112–13.

4. Ibid., p. 112.

5. "No Single Regulator for Banks," *Wall Street Journal*, December 15, 1993.

6. Peter Drucker, *Management* (New York: Harper and Row, 1985), p. 479.

7. Ibid., p. 499.

8. Ibid., p. 126.

9. Daniel Yergin and Thane Gustafson, *Russia 2010: And What It Means for the World* (New York: Random House, 1993), p. 8.

10. Ibid., p. 11.

11. Ibid.

12. Ibid., p. 9.

13. Ibid., p. 12.

14. "The Man with the Midas Touch Meets His Match in the Nation's Steakhouses," *Wall Street Journal*, January 3, 1994.

15. Von Mises, *Human Action*, p. 116.

16. "Die and Let Live," North Texas Public Broadcasting, written and produced by Shelia Coope, 1993; emphasis added.

17. Edward de Bono, *Teaching Thinking* (New York: Penguin, 1991), pp. 72–73.

18. Nathaniel Branden, *The Psychology of Self-Esteem* (New York: Bantam, 1971), p. 126; emphasis added.

19. *NBC Nightly News*, September 27, 1993.

20. *NBC Nightly News*, October 11, 1993.

21. Richard E. Neustadt and Ernest R. May, *Thinking in Time: The Uses of History for Decision-Makers* (New York: Macmillan, 1986), p. 137.

22. Ibid., p. 136; emphasis added.

23. Ibid., p. 81.

24. Ibid., p. 170.

25. Ibid., p. 79; emphasis in original.

26. Ibid., p. 89.

27. "How Morgan Stanley Maps Its Moves," *Institutional Investor* (June 1992): p. 53

28. Ibid., p. 52.

29. Ibid.

POSTSCRIPT

1. Howard Banks, *The Rise and Fall of Freddie Laker* (London: Faber and Faber, 1982), pp. 9–10, 105–7.

2. "Steve Jobs's Vision, So Right at Apple, Now Is Falling Short: Deep Faith in His Own Genius," *Wall Street Journal*, May 25, 1993.

3. "Roy Raymond's Life and Death Yield Grim Case Study: Suicide of Founder of Victoria's Secret Followed Failure to Regain Glory," *Wall Street Journal*, September 29, 1993.

4. Mark Pendergrast, *For God, Country, and Coca-Cola: The Definitive History of the Great American Soft Drink and the Company That Makes It* (New York: Macmillan, 1993), p. 342.

5. Ibid., p. 347.

6. Ibid., p. 350.

7. Ibid., p. 351.

8. Ibid., p. 353.

9. Ibid., p. 359.

10. Ibid., p. 355.

11. "Sahlman Says," *Wall Street Journal*, October 15, 1993.

12. "What Makes a Good Salesman," in *Business Classics: Fifteen Key Concepts for Managerial Success* (Cambridge, Mass.: Harvard Business Review, 1952), pp. 52–53.

13. John Dickhaut, "Escalation Errors and the Sunk Cost Effect: An Explanation Based on Reputation and Information Asymmetries," *Journal of Accounting Research* 27 (Spring 1989): pp. 59–77.

14. "Just What Is an Entrepreneur?" *Business Week*, Bonus Issue: Enterprise, October 1993, pp. 105–6.

15. "Would You Believe It? Craig McCaw Says He Is Risk Averse," *Forbes*, March 1, 1993, p. 79.

16. Ibid., p. 80; emphasis added.

17. Ed Zschau, review of *Steve Jobs and the NeXT Big Thing*, by Randall E. Stross, *Wall Street Journal*, December 10, 1993.

18. "Talented Outcasts: Bear Stearns Prospers Hiring Daring Traders That Rival Firms Shun," *Wall Street Journal*, November 11, 1993.

19. An Wang, *Lessons: An Autobiography* (Reading, Mass.: Addison Wesley, 1986), p. 1.

BIBLIOGRAPHY

Banks, Howard. *The Rise and Fall of Freddie Laker*. London: Faber and Faber, 1982.

Branden, Nathaniel. *The Psychology of Self-Esteem*. New York: Bantam, 1971.

De Bono, Edward. *Teaching Thinking*. New York: Penguin, 1991.

Drucker, Peter. *Management*. New York: Harper and Row, 1985.

Epstein, Richard A. *The Theory of Gambling and Statistical Logic*. New York: Academic Press, 1977.

Gann, W. D. *How to Make Profits in Commodities*. Pomeroy, Wash.: Lambert-Gann, 1951.

Hazlitt, Henry. *The Failure of the "New Economics": An Analysis of the Keynesian Fallacies* Lanham, Md.: University Press of America, 1983.

Janus, Irving L. *Victims of Groupthink: A Psychological Study of Foreign-Policy Decisions and Fiascoes*. Boston: Houghton Mifflin, 1972.

Kindleberger, Charles, P. *Manias, Panics, and Crashes: A History of Financial Crises*. New York: Basic, 1989.

Kübler-Ross, Elisabeth. *On Death and Dying*. New York: Macmillan, 1969.

Le Bon, Gustave. *The Crowd: A Study of the Popular Mind*. New York: The Macmillan Co., 1896.

Mackay, Charles. *Extraordinary Popular Delusions and the Madness of Crowds*. Boston: L.C. Page, 1932.

Mises, Ludwig von. *Human Action: A Treatise on Economics*. Chicago: Contemporary, 1966.

Neil, Humphrey. *The Art of Contrary Thinking*. Caldwell, Idaho: Caxton Printers, 1954.

Neustadt, Richard E., and Ernest R. May, *Thinking in Time: The Uses of History for Decision-Makers*. New York: Macmillan, 1986.

Pendergrast, Mark. *For God, Country, and Coca-Cola: The Definitive History of the Great American Soft Drink and the Company That Makes It*. New York: Macmillan, 1993.

Schwager, Jack. *Market Wizards: Interviews with Top Traders*. New York: New York Institute of Finance, 1989.

Shubik, Martin. *The Uses and Methods of Gaming*. New York: Elsevier, 1978

Smitely, Robert. *Popular Financial Delusions*. Burlington, Vt.: Fraser, 1963.

Talley, Madelon DeVoe. *The Passionate Investors*. New York: Crown, 1987.

Thorp, Edward O. *Beat the Dealer: A Winning Strategy for the Game of Twenty-one*. New York: Vintage, 1966.

Train, John. *The New Money Masters*. New York: Harper and Row, 1989.

Wang, An. *Lessons: An Autobiography*. Reading, Mass.: Addison Wesley, 1986.

Yergin, Daniel, and Thane Gustafson. *Russia 2010: And What It Means for the World*. New York: Random House, 1993.